T0079694

OFFAL

Edible

Series Editor: Andrew F. Smith

EDIBLE is a revolutionary new series of books dedicated to food and drink that explores the rich history of cuisine. Each book reveals the global history and culture of one type of food or beverage.

Already published

Apple Erika Janik *Beef* Lorna Piatti-Farnell *Bread* William Rubel *Cake* Nicola Humble *Caviar* Nichola Fletcher *Champagne* Becky Sue Epstein *Cheese* Andrew Dalby *Chocolate* Sarah Moss and Alexander Badenoch *Cocktails* Joseph M. Carlin *Curry* Colleen Taylor Sen *Dates* Nawal Nasrallah *Gin* Lesley Jacobs Solmonson *Hamburger* Andrew F. Smith *Herbs* Gary Allen *Hot Dog* Bruce Kraig *Ice Cream* Laura B. Weiss *Lemon* Toby Sonneman *Lobster* Elisabeth Townsend *Milk* Hannah Velten *Offal* Nina Edwards *Olive* Fabrizia Lanza *Oranges* Clarissa Hyman *Pancake* Ken Albala *Pie* Janet Clarkson *Pizza* Carol Helstosky *Pork* Katharine M. Rogers *Potato* Andrew F. Smith *Rum* Richard Foss *Sandwich* Bee Wilson *Soup* Janet Clarkson *Spices* Fred Czarra *Tea* Helen Saberi *Whiskey* Kevin R. Kosar *Wine* Marc Millon

Offal

A Global History

Nina Edwards

REAKTION BOOKS

Published by Reaktion Books Ltd
33 Great Sutton Street
London EC1V ODX, UK
www.reaktionbooks.co.uk

First published 2013

Printed and bound in China by C&C Offset Printing Co., Ltd

British Library Cataloguing in Publication Data
Edwards, Nina
Offal : a global history. – (Edible)
1. Variety meats. 2. Cooking (Variety meats) – History.
I. Title II. Series
641.3´6-DC23

ISBN 978 1 78023 097 9

Contents

Introduction 7
1 Definitions and Ideas 15
2 The Offal Tradition 30
3 The West 43
4 Macho Status 70
5 As Ritual 87
6 As Medicine 99
7 Leftovers 106

Recipes 109
References 121
Select Bibliography 130
Websites and Associations 134
Acknowledgements 135
Photo Acknowledgements 136
Index 137

Introduction

In the beginning there was offal. Offal – organ or variety meat, entrails or viscera, innards and extremities – has been eaten since man first hunted down prey. It can be brazenly meaty or subtle and refined. Consumed all over the world, it exists both as staple food and sought-after delicacy. Even before we had fire to cook with, inner organs were easier to consume, cut straight from the newly killed animal, more palatable raw than muscle meat, yielding to the teeth and still warm with life. Lean, wild animals store valuable fats within their inner organs. The extra surge of energy these hidden parts provide fuelled the hunter, wholly reliant for survival on personal strength and stamina.

Aboriginal food cultures that have survived to this day provide some understanding of what and how early man ate, and provide evidence to support the idea that offal would have been a valued food that was eaten raw, held over an open fire or baked in mud in the embers. The advent of fire meant it was possible to combine the qualities of taste and texture of different cuts of meat, muscle and offal. Gradually, with the use of pelt receptacles and, later, clay pots, it became possible to boil and stew meat, infusing it with seasoning, herbs and spices. Arable farming brought a greater range of cereals and vegetables to the pot. Raising livestock meant that dairy products could be used and meat could be bred. Domestic animals could be relatively sedentary, kept safe from predators, allowing their internal organs to grow large, fed with grain and cultivated grasses, depending on the culinary purpose they were to serve.

From tomb paintings we can gain some insight into what offal was eaten in ancient Egypt and how it was prepared. Food left for the mummified dead includes heart, which was believed to be a source of strength for the departed, and evidence of cooked kidneys has also been found.[1] The fact that liver is the most accepted form of offal today owes much to ancient Egyptians noticing that geese would feed themselves up before their long migrations. Those caught and eaten during such periods were found to have abnormally large livers,

Sheep offal stewed in a huge casserole with lots of onions, a few herbs, olive oil and white wine and served with yogurt. In Greece and the rest of the Middle East more spices tend to be used than in this Cypriot dish.

Maydum geese, Egypt, *c.* 2620 BC, from the tomb of Nefermaat and Itet. Further paintings show the geese being force-fed pellets of bread, dates and oil to enrich and enlarge their livers.

and so the practice of cramming birds was born.[2] Painted geese, ducks and cranes process around the walls of the tomb of Ti, a high-ranking official from the end of the Egyptian Fifth Dynasty (2498–2345 BC), now housed in the Louvre. The reliefs were taken from a chamber showing other types of food preparation, and significantly scribes are shown recording the servants' methods, perhaps confirming the existence of early recipes. Small sausages of dough are being hand-rolled and arranged ceremonially in gilded vessels. The birds' necks are then massaged to encourage them to swallow the food. Liquid, probably oil, is poured into their bills to help them swallow. The birds seem to be queueing up, stretching their wings in apparent anticipation. Offal husbandry is shown to be an elaborate skill, and liver a food fit for an important landowner, worthy as sustenance for the afterlife.

There is written evidence of offal consumption from the times of classical antiquity. Accounts from the chronicler

Athenaeus (fl. *c.* AD 300) and the physician Galen (*c.* AD 129-199) bring to life the beginnings of fine eating, with offal at its decadent centre. The Spartans' severe warrior society relied on a rich pork broth, infused with blood before battle.[3] The pig was the most widely eaten and affordable animal, with the breasts and uteri of young sows considered a particular delicacy. Hippocrates (*c.* 460 BC–270 BC) and Galen both refer to ox liver and there is evidence of a wide range of animal and fish innards and extremities being enjoyed, in the comedies of Aristophanes, for example, and in banqueting-scene illustrations on black- and red-figure vases.[4] While the ancient Greeks may have tended towards a frugal diet, and food preparation was so disregarded as to allow even women to cook, the influence of the Persian diet, rich in fruit, nuts, spices and offal, meant that the wealthy at least were open to more elaborate food. There is something about offal, in its relation to our own bodies, that appeals to those seeking luxury and excess.

Fattened goose liver is referred to by the Greek poet Archestratus (mid-fourth 4th century BC) as 'the soul of the goose'.[5] Birds that had been fattened were thought suitable political gifts between Athens and Sparta. The Roman statesman Cato describes the Roman process of force-feeding geese and ducks with balls of moistened cereal.[6] The birds were sometimes fed with pounded figs to tenderize them, and sometimes with honeyed wine, which was also given to sows to improve their livers. Pliny the Elder recommends soaking livers, once extracted, in milk and honey, to make them larger and sweeter.[7] This early foie gras was often served hot, according to the Roman poet Juvenal. The livers of red mullet, or surmullet, were also something of a craze, valued for their delicate flavour.

Greeks and Romans prepared black pudding from ox blood. *Apicius*, a book of Roman recipes from the late fourth

In ancient Rome goose liver pâté was highly valued. This French *pâté de foie gras* is enriched with truffles and cranberries.

or early fifth century BC, includes directions for making a pudding in which the blood is thickened with chopped boiled egg yolks, onions, leeks and pine kernels, though more everyday puddings would have used cereal; it is stuffed into intestines rather than stomach lining.[8] *Botulus*, a type of blood sausage, was sold on the streets of Rome. Boiled tripe was another typical dish. In the *Iliad* Andromache's laments for her son's future after the death of Hector are voiced in terms of the offal he will no longer be offered to eat: 'Once he fed on marrow only and the fat of lamb.' This 'fat of lamb' refers to the fat-tailed sheep, which stores fat reserves in its rump or tail and is mentioned in Leviticus (3:1–11) as an offering. Nowadays around 25 per cent of all sheep are fat-tailed breeds, which are found mostly in arid regions of southeast Europe, North Africa and Asia.

Lungs were eaten but kidneys were less popular. Brains were a delicacy, Aristotle referring to them as widely eaten and Galen recommending them for health,[9] but they could be contentious. Pythagoras and his followers avoided brain and heart because of a belief that the souls of the dead could migrate to other creatures, and that these were parts of particular significance to the individual.[10] However, the modest appetites of the Pythagorians contrast with the more affluent reaches of ancient Greek society, and even more so with the excesses of Roman gastronomy.

Offal can be a monitor of class distinction. Larks, thrushes, nightingales and flamingos were hunted for Roman emperors for their tongues alone, an example of sumptuous consumption. Seneca remonstrates against the 'monstrous sybaritic excesses of those who select only certain portions of an animal out of disgust for the rest'.[11] But this distaste betrays the strength of the Roman appetite for such foodstuffs. *Apicius* mentions smoked pig's liver sausages wrapped in caul and bay leaves, and brain forcemeat formed into little dumplings with lovage, oregano, pepper and eggs, bound together with stock. Fish sauce, or *garum*, was made from mackerel intestines fermented over several months, and is similar to the *nam pla* fish sauce of Southeast Asia. *Garum* was used so widely that it tended to mask more subtle tastes, part of a wider vogue for concealing the true identity of what was being served. This might in turn be seen as a forerunner of much twentieth-century offal cuisine, in which elaborate sauces were intended to predominate and conceal what lay beneath as if protecting the sensibilities of the diner.

Stories purporting to describe the behaviour of Emperor Elagabalus, a figure of voluptuous extravagance, portray offal as a symbol of his intemperate appetites. An admirer of *Apicius*, he is said to have eaten 'camel heels, cockscombs, the tongues of peacocks and nightingales, the brains of flamingos and thrushes . . . and the heads of parrots and pheasants, and the beards of mullets.'[12] The tongues may have been in part to protect him from plague, but the cockscombs both have rarity-appeal and add the frisson to be gained from slicing the combs from live birds at table. Elagabalus dallied with status by lavishing precious goose liver on his dogs, and for

Jan Baptist Weenix, *Pig's Carcase*, 1647–61, oil on canvas.

30 days he is said to have treated his servants to the elevated
dish of pregnant sow's udder, a dish usually kept for high
priests and emperors alone. He loved to throw unusual banquets, with slaves and palace servants enjoying prodigious
amounts of the viscera of mullet, flamingos and thrushes, the
heads of parrots and pheasants, and peacock brains.

The lower ranks of society not so indulged might have
eaten tripe,[13] blood or the heads of sheep – which Juvenal

calls, with a touch of bathos, 'a feast fit for a cobbler' – but their recipes go unrecorded. Mireille Corbier imagines the aspirations of a slave of the lowest order, who longed to taste again the sow's womb he once ate in a tavern.[14]

In the ancient world offal was widely eaten, and it could be something to aspire to, a dish suggesting luxury. During the Renaissance there was a revival of interest in extravagant offal dishes, and the recipes of the great eighteenth- and nineteenth-century French chefs used offal in fantastical cuisine. Not until the recent revival for nose to tail eating in the West has offal been so highly regarded.

I

Definitions and Ideas

What might the term 'offal' include? The *Chambers Dictionary*'s definition sounds a little less than enthusiastic: 'waste or rejected parts esp. of a carcass: an edible part cut off in dressing a carcass, esp. entrails, heart, liver, kidney, tongue etc.: anything worthless or unfit for use.'[1] Other edible innards not specified here include connective tissue, bone marrow, lungs, spleen, sweetbreads, testicles, udders, tripe, heads and the features thereof (brains, eyes, cheeks, snout or muzzle and ears), skin, tails, trotters, lard and blood. Offal is sometimes thought of as inner organs and viscera alone, but I include all edible exterior parts. In markets across the globe offal is openly displayed alongside livestock and carcasses. However, the colourful posters displayed in some Western butchers' shops, showing the division of available cuts, rarely include offal, suggesting there is sometimes a need for diplomacy – even secrecy – about eating such body parts.

The terms we use can be gently euphemistic, as in melt or milt for spleen; lights for lungs; brawn or headcheese for brains; crackling for crisp skin; and prairie oysters, mountain tendergroins, cowboy caviar, rocky mountains, fries and swinging beef for testicles. Bath chap refers to pig cheek and lower and sometimes upper jaw; chitterlings or chitlings are

Most probably used to advertise available cuts, this wooden model of a butcher's shop, *c.* 1850, is now a reminder of how meat was once commonly sold.

Paul Sandby, *Any Tripe or Neats or Calves Feet…*, part of a series of etchings, *Twelve London Cries Done from Life*, 1760. Ragged and careworn, the vendor wheels his barrow of calves' feet and other parts, calling out for business.

intestines; haslet is a loaf of pig offal; chine is backbone; faggots are offal balls; and Gaelic drisheen is a pudding of sheep intestine stuffed with blood and cereal.[2] Sometimes one body part is presented as another, as when testicles are termed sweetbreads (the correct term for pancreas or thymus gland) or kidneys in the case of cockerel's testes, *rognons blanc* in

French.[3] Sometimes the nomenclature for offal is disturbingly graphic or biological, as with udder, penis, birth canal and bladder. All sound like they come from some familiar doggerel, replete with medical, pornographic and *Carry On* film-style suggestiveness. Offal can seem both childishly smutty and too grown-up. Even the terminology used by the butchery trade can obfuscate, as when penis is termed pizzle.

These lists are not exhaustive, but demonstrate the size and range of the subject. The ingredient parts form a complex chain in the anatomy of beasts and inevitably recall our own physical, meaty make-up. It is possible, it is said, to eat all but the feathers or fur, talons and teeth. All but the squeal of the pig.

Perhaps there is some inherent meaning in the word. itself. 'Offal' suggests what falls off or away after the animal is slaughtered and what is left after the butcher has taken his prime cuts: the inner parts of an animal, that stew of slippery organs, glands, vessels, blood and tissue. Thus the term can suggest something that is less important, being only a byproduct of the butcher's art. Hieatt and Butler, in their medieval cookbook, quote a recipe from Arundel where the verbal connotation is latent: 'Take *garbage* of capons, and of hennes, and of chekyns, and of dowes, and make hem clene' (my italics). This suggests that offal is inferior to other meat and should be discarded as of no value, even as something dirty and disease-ridden. Shakespeare refers to rotting bodies as offal in *Hamlet* (II, 2): 'I should have fatted all the region kites/ With this slave's offal.'

The word 'offal' is etymologically linked with *afval* in Dutch, the German *Abfall* or *Offall*, *avfall* in Norwegian and Swedish, *affald* in Danish and *abats* in French. All of these words imply rubbish or animal waste and do not necessarily refer to food.

The word is a gift to the comedian. A number of offal-related words, such as giblets, sweetbreads and tripe, have become part of the comedian's lexicon; our laughter betrays our unease. In Yorkshire fat men are sometimes affectionately called Giblets. The heavy metal bands Offal and Necrophagist draw on offal's associated vocabulary and imagery in their lyrics, with 'Fermented Offal Discharge' a hit for the latter. *Offal News*, a political and economic blog, and TV *Offal*, a UK Channel 4 sketch show of the late 1990s, borrow offal's inherent sense of subversion to suggest satire. It can also be a term of abuse. To be 'de-offaled' has become a metaphor for distress, more graphic than 'gutted'. The word 'offal' is also used for the leftover scraps in glass-cutting and for fabric remnants too small to be of further use.

The sound of the word is rounded and soft on the palate, phonetically minor in key. It could be said to make

Ruth Dupré, *Butchery*, 2010, sculpture. Heavy, glistening glass ox tongue forms fall from a butcher's block.

The varied textures of tripe, from silky seersucker to mohair blanket.

a seductive shape in the mouth: the open vowel; the gentler sound of the 'ff'; the pleasing closure of the 'l'. Nonetheless, the accident that 'offal' can be homophonous with 'awful' contributes to some of the negative or comic associations the word invites.

Raw offal can seem more raw, more visceral than other meat, reminding us of a time before cooking, when early man tore into bloody prey. It suggests the crazed or defiant, like Diogenes and his alleged diet of raw flesh and creepy-crawlies. The challenge of offal comes alive in a description of learning to cook in China. Fuchsia Dunlop is determined to enjoy the 'silken strands' and 'tender flesh' of fish eyes, yet cannot help but empathize with her father's reluctance as he masticates 'rubbery goose intestine'.[4]

The extra-meatiness of offal is often part of the appeal. Next to the chewy, gristly, bloodily robust offal, other meats can seem insipid. Some avoid offal because it seems uglier than other cuts; conversely, some baulk at the idea of eating the inner parts of cute animals that remind us all too easily of ourselves and our own fragile bodies.

From tongue and beak in Sichuan Province to gizzard stew on the streets of Rio de Janeiro, from elegant Parisian *bonnes bouches* to spicy cartilage in the dust bowl of Calcutta, nose to tail eating is widespread. Offal is a food which represents the most elevated *haute cuisine* and yet also celebrates the ingenuity of the poverty-stricken. In France offal is still referred to as *les parties nobles* ('the noble pieces'). Italians deem offal *la cucina povera*, the food of the poor, its many age-old and more refined dishes springing from necessity, as in Douglas Houston's poem 'With the Offal Eaters': 'putting each beast killed to its full use / Their wives chop offal finely twice a week.'[5]

Most of the world eats offal. The cuisines of the Middle and Far East and Africa have always appreciated its qualities, while the great chefs of North America and Europe may rejoice in new opportunities to raise awareness of the culinary potential of these meats. The question remains whether ideas about 'real' food, advocated by American chef Chris Cosentino and Pierre Orsi in France, represent anything more than a fantasy – albeit an ambiguous and highly charged one – for the West. It may be that these ideas fail to affect day-to-day food choices. Moreover, there is a marked distinction between those who dress offal up in creamy sauces or combine it with non-offal meats as if to mask its identity, disguising its natural form, texture and scent, and those who prefer, like Fergus Henderson in his St John restaurant near Smithfield Market in London, to lay offal bare: with, say, suckling pig's brains served simply and without camouflage.

The writer and philosopher Roger Scruton describes food as having 'meaning, not just nourishment'. Because offal takes many forms, and attitudes to it vary in different cultures and within different income groups, its meanings are enmeshed. Its recipes, tastes, smells and textures, history and cultural context all exist against a backdrop – in the affluent West at least – of uncertainty over whether this is stuff we ought to eat. In cultures that until recently enjoyed offal, the better-off classes are beginning to reduce their consumption of it, while – conversely – many a gourmet or chef in the West encourage us to return to offal. Attitudes to offal, and remembered impressions of it, can be peculiarly complicated, but then so is offal itself. The rub here is between the physical sensations of taste, smell and appearance via our lips, mouths, taste buds and eyes, and our moral tastes or preferences. The food writer Tara Austen Weaver struggles with the idea:

> I think offal is far more intimidating than simply meat. Offal is foreboding, the nasty bits that many people prefer to avoid. In some way it is the essence of the animal – intestines, kidney, heart.[6]

The ways in which offal-associated vocabulary is used and the metaphors that surround it are illuminating. The fourteenth-century theory of bodily humours has invaded our ways of expressing internal life, forging a connection between physical organs and their hidden functions: one can be splenetic, choleric, liverish, phlegmatic or even just sadly melancholic. I may be lily-livered if I am gutless, heartless when I am not heartfelt. One suffers from heartburn or a chill on the kidneys. The edition of *Brewer's Dictionary of Phrase and Fable* of 1870 sourly informs us that veins or kidneys 'were even by the Jews supposed to be the seat of the affections'.

There exists a lexicon of words and phrases that appear to draw on our associations with offal, and suggest in turn how we have come to think of it. You may consider this to be a load of tripe, with not enough gristle, a bloody mess, brainless. Even archaic expressions can affect current attitudes. Blister my kidneys! I must keep my head, trust to my palate, be true to my heart's core, whether or not we are of the same kidney. Consider the extraneous offal parts and all their everyday comparative uses, which make eating their animal parities seem disturbingly intimate: keep your nose/snout out of it, keep your eyeballs peeled, your tail between your legs, your skin on, your ears flapping, heart's blood, in the recesses of your visceral maw, yet hold your tongue, for I never intended to seem tongue in cheek.

Given the backdrop of our relationship to offal and its associated vocabulary, any desire to imagine our own insides as a neat arrangement of organs and tubes like a child's model or a biology diagram at school, or just the wish to avoid thinking of ourselves as entrails encased in muscle and skin, is disrupted by our encounter with this foodstuff. We have a very limited idea of what lies inside our bodies. Jonathan Miller describes how what we think we know is often pastiche: 'We reconstruct our insides from pictures in advertisements for patent medicines, from half-remembered school science, from pieces of offal on butcher's slabs and all sorts of medical folklore.'[7] The resulting confusion may account in part for the curious impression that offal can make. In Edinburgh, chocolatier Nadia Ellingham sells haggis-flavoured chocolate: one suspects that it is popular not only for the blend of spices used, but also because the idea of meaty innards and chocolate creates a sense of pleasing disjuncture (though the chocolates contain no actual offal meat). The punning *Glasgow Herald* headline is revealing: 'Haggis Chocolate Does Not Taste Offal.'

Often people claim distaste for offal without having eaten it. Fermented fish offal, for example, is sometimes criticized because it smells and tastes of cat urine, and yet it is unlikely that many would ever have knowingly tasted the latter. For some the notion of fish innards is unappealing. It seems to be something other than the taste or smell that is off-putting. We tend to fear unexpected sensation. One might claim to like or dislike puréed celery, yet this has none of the force of an aversion to offal, and it might seem odd to feel contempt for someone who likes it or shame for liking it oneself. This reluctance to eat offal in particular is sometimes betrayed by the sort of apologies made by enthusiasts. Mary Douglas comments that 'the palate is trained [and] that taste and smell are subject to cultural control'.[8] While there is a complex range of reactions to foods we find difficult, there does seem to be a difference between disliking animal as opposed to vegetable matter.

Umami (the word means 'delicious taste' in Japanese), the fifth quality of taste besides bitter, salty, sour and sweet, is a complex savoury flavour that is significant in offal as well as being found in green tea, truffles, tomatoes, asparagus and some cheeses. Chinese cookery has long used a form of *umami*, or *wei jing*, otherwise known as MSG or monosodium glutamate. It is found in soy sauce and fermented fish sauce, and is a recognized flavour in Japan, Vietnam, Thailand and much of the Far East. Containing proteins and amino acids, it is high in the glutamates we first taste in mother's milk, creating a pleasing sensation in the mouth and making food seem more satisfying.

Offal also has other qualities that are familiar to us from other foods: saltiness, fattiness or a rich mouth-coating creaminess, as in brain and sweetbreads, and a metallic quality, as in blood or urine in kidneys. Such taste impressions may compete with one another, so that we notice the slightly acrid taste of ox liver, set off by the odour of its cooking, and find ourselves immune to – or perhaps drawn to – its savoury allure. In recent years the tasty threesome of sugar, salt and fat in Western diet has tended to dominate our food, rather than more subtle spice flavours, and this blunting of our facility to distinguish other tastes might be extended to the subtleties of offal *umami*.

Sometimes a dislike of eating offal is put down to its lack of definable form, even though the outer flesh of an animal, once eviscerated, is no more discrete. Spam, despite its joke acronyms such as 'spare parts animal meat', is still widely consumed by many who profess never to eat offal. The same might be said of some sausages and other processed meat products. In *yakitori* bars throughout modern Japan you will find skewers of distinctively flavoured chicken meat that are in fact parson's nose, that fleshy protuberance at the mouth of the anus that contains the fatty uropygial gland. If a foreigner questions the restaurant, she may be assured they are no such thing, the staff forearmed against a Westerner's distaste.

Perhaps it is the relation between offal and its living functions, its relation to blood, urine and faecal matter, that disturbs us. When we are short of breath our lungs make a ragged sound, so Elizabeth David's recollection of 'the sound of air gruesomely whistling through sheep's lungs frying in oil', or rattling through the valves of tripe, may seem too human to provoke our appetites.[9] Kidneys may disturb because their main function is to filter impurities and drain waste into the bladder. I am a thing, like all animals, whose mouth – with which I might speak, eat, kiss or sing arias of great beauty – is, in due course, connected to an anus.

Offal mainly comes from within the animal, suggesting a parallel with what we think of as our inner selves. My offal is my vitals, essential to life. My innermost being is the intimate marrow of what it is to think and feel, and thus it is sometimes troubling to think of eating entrails, guts, sexual parts or facial features.

Elaborate cleansing rites suggest that we may consider offal dirtier than other meat. On the one hand, waste matter needs to be removed, and on the other this requirement has become ritualized. Mrs Beeton goes to some lengths to stress the importance of hot blanching and further soakings in several changes of water in the preparation of various offal dishes. Weltering, or steeping, is intended to release flavour and remove impurities; blanching may whiten the food, neutralize any bacteria or enzymes present and delay the process of decay. Offal may also be soaked in milk, as if to take on its essential nurturing quality. The water used to clean the offal may be salted. In Japan this links to a traditional belief that elemental sea water is a purifying force.

The American and British obsession with the bowels might account for anxieties about eating animal guts. However, Jonathan Miller mentions that though the French are obsessed with their livers, there is little evidence that this inhibits their appetite for foie gras.[10]

We have become distanced from the processes of butchery and slaughterhouse in the West since the gradual movement from rural to urban living in the nineteenth century. Today meat is often packaged into neat portions that no longer remind us of its origins. Offal cannot always be so easily disguised. A frilly piece of sheep's tripe or a pair of pig's ears are all too redolent of their former role.

Cooks and gourmets promote offal in terms of its flavour and value for money. In the same breath they speak

Brilliantly dyed pickled ox tail, Brixton Market, South London.

of prime cuts as being first-class meats, implying that offal is not of this rank. Yet when Fergus Henderson describes deep-fried lamb's brains as 'like biting through crunch into a rich cloud' he not only evokes the paradoxical changes in texture from crisp to suddenly delicate and insubstantial, but appeals to some transcendental quality of the taste experience.[11]

2

The Offal Tradition

Most of the world has never had a problem with offal. On the contrary, it is at the meaty core of many cultures' gastronomy. In China's age-old regional cuisine, offal allows even the poorest to elevate a meal from eating to live to something more choice. Pork blood soup and offal dumplings, or *jiaozi*, were eaten by night labourers in Kaifeng over 1,000 years ago. Offal-enriched dumplings have long been eaten in both Russia and Turkey. Today the largest market of the United States, a major exporter of offal, is China, for their pork feet, tongue and heart.[1] Offal is food for all, adding flavour and texture to the scantiest diet. In the late thirteenth century Marco Polo observed poor people in the province of Carajan in Mongolia eating raw liver straight from the carcass: they 'cut it small, and put it in a sauce of garlic and spices, and so eat it'.[2]

The *Li-Chi* or *Book of Rites* lists liver as a great delicacy, suitable sustenance for the elderly, and suggests a relation between the freshness of food and good health. Offal, which must be eaten fresh, if not raw, is therefore recommended as a healthy food.

Offal is basic food on the streets of China and at the same time harks back to imperial court cuisine. Pork offal predominates. Intestines and uterus are particularly valued, but the offal of chicken, geese, duck and cattle is also enjoyed. This ancient fast food can be marinated and then cooked in moments. Dishes using pork include liver slices fried with onions or floating in clear broth; pork braised in sweetened soy, or *wu xiang*, served cold; and deep fried pork intestine, *zha fei chang*, dipped in fermented *tian mian jiang* Sichuan sauce. *Lo mei* are little offal snacks that have become something of a fashion in New York restaurants of late. All parts of the poultry are used, including the feet and the tongue as well as hearts and livers. Several ducks' tongues are served on a plate, usually fried. A feast of duck's head, halved and served with tongue alongside it, is a delicacy dating back 600 years to the Ming Dynasty. Chicken's feet are a popular snack. An American English-language teacher on a boat journey from Shanghai to Texas with a group of Chinese tried to acclimatize herself

Chicken's feet, deep-fried, stewed or barbecued, are a great delicacy in many cultures where the texture of skin and tendon are appreciated.

to this food: 'Each foot had long, skinny toes, and each toe had a tiny, oval nail on the end. The joints, where the skin wrinkled, looked like human knuckles.'[3]

Offal dishes vary by region in China, both in preparation methods and in what is available. Shandong excels in seafood offal and tripe dishes, whereas Cantonese cooking places more of an emphasis on pork and beef, and traditionally dog and snake offal. Sichuan cuisine is spicy, seasoned with chilli, cayenne, Sichuan pepper and ginger. A typically hot, spiced stew of pork kidneys, *wu gen chang wang*, contains blood cakes and tofu, and is said to keep out the cold. Blood tofu, or *pin yin*, is made from duck's blood and served with sticky rice. Pork tongue sliced in sesame oil is another typical Sichuan dish in the melee of delicate or robust, hot and spicy or subtly distinct additions to a diet based on rice and noodles. Yet

A Chinese stall crammed with dried offal including dried pig's snout and larynx.

Salmon fish heads with their delicate scarlet gills are used to make soup in Japan, flavoured with ginger and *kombu* seaweed. The cheeks are especially prized for their meaty texture and intense flavour.

though offal sometimes plays the role of a luxury food in China, Fuchsia Dunlop reflects that *chao ji za*, for example, is a stir-fried dish of chicken parts that would be thrown away by most European cooks.[4]

For the inexperienced Westerner, the most off-putting aspect of offal as it is prepared in the East can be its challenging texture. For example, the ancient custom of serving the head of a fish to an honoured guest relies on its being newly killed to keep tender the delicate flesh of the jowls and eyes.[5] Fish heads are considered a dish fit for royalty in Thailand, served with caramel sauce.[6] Pork kidneys are recognized as being nourishing and the suet fat that surrounds them is considered healthy and easily digestible. For the Chinese palate the unusual texture is something to be savoured, setting it apart from the bland food of the West. Crispiness and a certain chewiness might be acceptable but the taste for gristle and things that slip and gloop in the mouth can be hard to acquire.

In South Korea sliced cows' feet are used for a spicy soup that might once have been made with indigenous buffalo. It is customary to serve guests a drink accompanied by small snacks, and these are traditionally offal, including chicken's feet and pig skin, ears and kidneys, usually presented on short wooden skewers. Texture is often considered more important than taste.[7] A popular dish consists of pork intestines stuffed with spiced noodles. It is kept soft, just holding together, for the experience of its sudden disintegration in the mouth.

In northeastern Thailand and Laos a raw – or almost raw – minced meat dish called *lu* (larb or larp) is dressed with entrails and the enzyme-rich stomach contents of the animal, which is usually deer. Sometimes the effect can be surprising to the uninitiated:

Larb lu, minced raw beef with blood, bile and spices on a Chiang Mai market stall.

Pho soup stall in a Hanoi street market. The broth is made from beef bone and oxtail, sometimes chicken, with slices of meat such as tripe and flavoured with a wide range of spices and herbs including charred ginger, cardamom, fennel, cinnamon, star anise, lime, chillies and fermented fish sauce.

'It's very nice, but it's bitter,' the young man observed, not knowing that the more bitter the larp the better.

'Of course it's bitter. It's delicious. I especially asked for the *di*.' *Di* was the green liquid which comes from a little sac adjacent to the liver.[8]

Soup can be a way of eking out small quantities of offal to to add flavour to a starch-based diet, such as in pig's organ soup, a traditional street food in Singapore. The past French colonial presence in Vietnam has led to fresh baguette sandwiches, or *banh mi*, stuffed with offal, fresh herbs, ginger and star anise, sometimes with pickled carrot and daikon. Rice porridge with pig offal, *cháo lòng*, and deep-fried pig intestines are popular street food.

The Japanese, historically a people that have relied on the sea for their survival, favour seafood offal, considering it particularly healthy. Among *chimni*, or 'rare taste' foods, are *ankimo* (monkfish liver), *mefun* (pickled liver and other internal organs of a male salmon) and *shiokara* (finely chopped seafood in a brown sauce made from its pulverized and fermented viscera). *Shiokara* is a popular snack; bars specializing in this delicacy might offer squid, oyster, shrimp or sea urchin varieties, often accompanied by whisky. Pickled sea cucumber innards, *konowata*, are prized for their slippery texture, and are known as *trepang* in Indonesia and *balatan* in the Philippines.

Offal from mammals, and in particular large animals, was considered unclean in Shinto terms, though today Japanese *yakitori* bars include beef as well as chicken offal. Cow's tongue is considered a delicacy. A mixed dish of offal is known in Kansai dialect as *horum onyaki*, or discarded goods, and thought to be particularly healthy. Beef or pork offal hotpot, *motsu nabe*, served with *ramen*, broth and noodles, can include larynx, spleen, birth canal, tongue, uterus, rectum, diaphragm and various bits of cartilage. If grilled on bamboo skewers over charcoal, the offal is served with a fiery mustard. *Motsu nabe* is best known for containing beef intestines and became less popular after the worldwide BSE outbreak, though a minority continue to seek it out, partly to defy such danger. A desire to shock often influences opulent Japanese cuisine, leading to dishes such as frog heart, still beating, as an expensive and esoteric sushi morsel.

Dinuguan blood sausage or stew (sometimes known as 'chocolate meat' because of its rich, dark colour) is a typical Filipino dish that contains pork intestine and ears, served hot and spicy. Indonesian *sambal goreng hati* is highly spiced with galangal, lime leaves, lemon grass, tamarind and shrimp paste and cooked with brown sugar, and *kemiri* is beef liver cooked with coconut milk until almost dry. In India and Pakistan,

A beef offal menu outside a Tokyo restaurant, with translations for the errant foreigner.

where meat is eaten every part is utilized. *Kata-kat* is a heavily spiced mixed offal dish usually of goat or chicken, and in the south of India a similar ragout uses pork, known as *rakhti*. Nepalese chicken gizzards are a highly prized delicacy.

In the Middle East couscous can be infused with offal. A medieval Arab rice dish, *Ibriing Majani*, is a gargantuan feast of 50 trotters and 20 sheep's heads.[9] Iranian food is rich in sheep offal, with kebabs made of liver, kidney, heart, brains and tongue served as traditional festive treats. Knee joints and sheep's tongues, known as *kale pache*, are traditional breakfast fare, and are served with beans and flatbread. Fish eyes – raw, boiled or deep fried – are found in traditional Lebanese and North African cuisine. Sheep intestines can be stuffed with rice. Anissa Helou recalls a Lebanon childhood eating 'raw liver for breakfast, stuffed tripe and intestines for lunch and fried testicles for dinner', though even she admits to a reluctance now to experience the rubbery texture of lungs.[10] It is the freshness of the meat, still blood-warm, that she remembers most fondly. Lamb brains – fresh, lightly cooked and folded inside flatbread – are fast food, but tripe and intestine, for example, need meticulous preparation, removing veins and vessels. It can be difficult to remove all traces of the meat's former life, but this echo can become part of the pleasure. Like a strong cheese, it is not the presence of mould that is savoured, but rather a flavoursome hint of decay.

The Balkans, straddling East and West, have a long tradition of whole-animal consumption. The Ottomans introduced *shkembe chorba*, a thick tripe soup, to Turkey; it is reputed to cure a hangover. In Turkey there are specialist tripe restaurants

Kokoretsi is a combination of sheep's liver, heart, lungs and fat skewered and wrapped in intestines, then wrapped again in suet and finally in more intestine. The resulting sausage is then grilled on charcoal.

or *i kembeci* where you can eat soup late into the night. During the Turkish feast of sacrifice, Kurban Bayrami, 'tripe soup is made without fail in every home where the ritual of sacrifice has been observed.'[11] Barbecued lamb and goat offal is sometimes wrapped in leaves and left in the embers to slow-cook; small intestines are eased over or wrapped around skewers of mixed offal which are then roasted on an open spit. In Greece *splinantero* is a spleen sausage and *kokoretsi* uses pluck (heart, liver and lungs). A similar sausage is known as *kokoreç* in Turkey, which can be served as an Easter dish. *Picti* is peppered pig's head brawn and braised calf's brains are wrapped in vine leaves to keep them moist. Cypriot *zalatina* brawn includes cracked pork trotters and is prepared with cinnamon bark and chillies, mixed with pork or lamb's tongue and seasoned with lemon and vinegar.[12] In Russia kidneys and tongue are traditionally served braised with gherkins and sweetened with sultanas and almonds. Calf's head with prune sauce, fried udder and brain patties are mentioned in Elena Molokhovets's *A Gift to Young Housewives* (1861). Armenian *khash*, made from animal feet and other parts, was once a food of the very poor, but is now considered a rare delicacy among the newly wealthy. It is considered to have more caché than, say, *yere pouni* brain fritters.

The evening meal, or *iftar*, during the Muslim holy month of Ramadan is a time of family get-togethers and includes simple dishes of cereal, vegetables and fruit enriched with small amounts of meat and offal in particular, though lately these evening meals have become more elaborate.[13] The three days at the end of the fasting period, known as Eid, are a time of celebration whose traditional dishes include stewed tripe and liver kebabs, and *boulfaf*, liver wrapped in caul and grilled. The most renowned offal in North Africa and the Middle East is lamb's head, casseroled in Algeria as *bouzellouf masli*.

An offal butchers in Iran, where offal remains a popular food. A traditional breakfast consists of sheep's tongue and knee joints, *kale pach*, served with beans and flatbread.

Arto der Haroutunian describes the nostalgic pull of the street hawkers' ancient cry, selling roasted lamb's heads.[14] He remarks that though they are no longer sold ready cooked, all offal parts are still widely available. Calf or lamb brains have been so long enjoyed that there is a common saying that 'too much sheep's brains make you sheepish'. Lamb's head soup is popular in the Middle East, Asia and the Mediterranean. In the ancient pre-Islamic Berber tradition, *harira* soup was enriched with liver and gizzards.

Mexican *enchilada* tortillas can be filled with all manner of offal; *antojitos* (little cravings), are a popular street food and come in many forms, such as *gorditas* (little fat ones) and corn-meal pastries stuffed with spicy liver or *huaraches*, wrapped round pieces of tongue.[15] Latin America gives us *chinchulines* and chitterlings, or *tripa gorda*, sweetbreads and marinated tongue, and ravioli stuffed with brains. Brazil has roasted offal parts, *feijoada* with pork trotters, tail and ears, gizzard and stomach stews. The Argentinian *asado* method of grilling, in which a whole lamb is spreadeagled over an open fire, has been adopted in Brazil, Chile, Paraguay and Uruguay. The *achuras* (offal) is served first, while it is still tender. In Latin America and the Caribbean *mondongo* soup is a hearty conflation of bone marrow and hoof jelly with tripe; it originated from the cuisine of African slaves in the Dominican Republic and Puerto Rico. In Venezuela tamarind and cassaba are added, and the dish is said to be so filling that it must be eaten either very early to fuel the day, or late in the evening before dancing. Offal has never fallen from grace in these cultures, and is recognized even in its most modest form for its rarity and flavour.

Elisabeth Luard in *The Latin American Kitchen* mentions 'the bits of the pig considered unfit for the master', which resulted in the Brazilian *feijoada* stew and fiery Caribbean pepperpot, which was originally offal-based.[16] Grenada has a traditional dish of tripe stew with onions and garlic, thought a nourishing food for children, that in Berlin or Paris would more likely be the food of the gastronome.

There are pockets of the developed West where offal is still enjoyed, not because it is fashionable, but because it remains an integral part of food culture, and that connection has never been broken. Some commentators trace a certain reticence towards variety meat-eating to its association with rationing after the Second World War. Yet societies that have kept true to offal have hardly been strangers to periods of famine followed by plenty. It is not so much affluence that has changed attitudes, but class. Thorstein Veblen's theory of conspicuous consumption in *The Theory of the Leisure Class* (1899) links status to the ability to be seen to be wasteful. The details of what you eat and how you prepare food are useful indicators of social standing. With the rise of a middle class, what people eat becomes a way of separating themselves from the lower orders – and the fact that offal is inexpensive and uses all parts of the animal associates it with lower-status living.

3
The West

Offal can excite extreme reactions. Nowadays in much of the West people tend to love it or hate it. Queen Victoria reputedly spooned up roasted bone marrow every day of her life. Some find the very mention of offal satisfying, exciting, even erotic. To divide the world into those cultures that still eat offal without hesitation and those that are markedly less enthusiastic is perhaps too clear a distinction. Yet reticence to eat offal – apart from liver and, to some extent, kidneys – has increased in the West along with the gradual emergence of an affluent middle class. A desire for separation from those of lower status meant that what people ate became an important indicator of class distinctions. Food became polarized into what was robust and traditional, on the one hand, and on the other finer cuisine, eaten by finer folk.

Historically offal was a natural part of the cuisines of America and Europe: chitterlings, a dish of German origin made of the intestines of pigs or other animals; potted meats; brawn and faggots wrapped in caul, the lacy membrane surrounding the inner organs. Europe's long tradition of eating offal forms part of the bedrock of American cuisine. Regional offal consumption survives across Canada and in the American South in particular. Minorities in America,

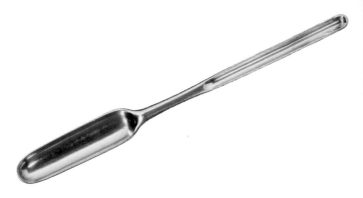

John Wirgman, bone marrow scoop, 1748–9, silver. This double-ended version allows the savoury fat to be extracted from both large and small bones.

Australia, New Zealand and throughout developed Europe have kept the art of offal cuisine alive, enriched by each new wave of immigration.

Today America is perhaps the world's least enthusiastic consumer of offal, but it was not always so. Early settlers – German, Dutch, Huguenot, Scottish, Welsh, Irish, Jewish, Swedish, African and English – brought with them their disparate culinary knowhow. The often harsh conditions and lack of refrigeration prohibited wastefulness. Settlers had to carry food on long treks into the new territories, but game offal could be foraged en route, including beaver tail, turkey, bear and buffalo in particular, which could be salted, pickled or smoked as a means of adding interest to basic supplies. Black puddings and various boiled suet puddings might be wrapped in intestine or caul. German and Dutch settlers brought with them a predilection for pork, introducing stomach, soused or marinated parts like pickled pig's feet, and scrapple (a loaf of scraps bound with corn meal).[1] Native Americans bartered offal with settlers, buffalo tongue being of high exchange value. Tongues could be salted and thousands of buffalo were killed for their delicacies alone: 'only the choicest parts were taken. The tongue, hump ribs and fleece fat were always included, as well as the marrow bones, and generally the gall and liver', explains Hiram Martin Chittenden in *The American Fur Trade of the Far West*.[2]

Exhausted hunters, too hungry to wait until they had got back to camp and built a fire, might eat the tenderest morsels raw. Others enjoyed the intestines and might swallow them by the yard, practically without chewing, though these were more usually lightly boiled.[3] Borrowed from the Native American diet, pemmican – a small cake made from dried meat, berries, dried fruit and bone marrow – was a survival food. It was adopted by fur traders and later by Arctic and Antarctic explorers.

Advertisement for foie gras by Leonetto Cappiello, *c.* 1928, with the crowned golden goose against a sumptuous red background, smiling down at the tinned pâté.

In the last 50 years offal has continued to be eaten as a regional speciality and is sometimes culturally specific, with fried brawn sandwiches in the Ohio River Valley, the Yiddish lungen stew, gribenes (chicken crackling) and chicken livers, scrapple among the Amish, and the typical Southern and Midwest dishes of gizzards and hog maw (stomach). Holding a barbecue, meat cooked in a pit, was a popular means of celebration in the Southern states and slaves might be given unwanted scraps of offal to supplement their meaner fare. Chitterlings became closely associated with the cultural identity of African Americans, a symbol of survival and pride. They are a marginal choice today, and though there may be core support for chitterlings, the survival of the practice of eating them relies in part on its shock factor.

The same is true of testicle eating. Regional Testicle Festivals in the USA started up in the 1980s.[4] Some organized events feature turkey testicles alone, as in Byron, Illinois, and some specialize in other types, as with the Testicle Festival in Oakdale, California, which celebrates bulls' testicles. They are sometimes served raw, but are more often boiled, sautéed or breaded and deep-fried.

There are also societies set up to support liver consumption. These not only try out more unusual dishes, such as liver mousse with puréed blackberries at the Regina Liver Lovers' Club, but enjoy traditional favourites such as liver and onions:

> Liver lovers tend to be older people who have rural roots – and mothers who knew how to cook it: soaked in milk, dipped in flour and quickly cooked . . . The U.S. produced 108,771 metric tons of edible liver in 2010, but it ships 89% overseas, most to Egypt.[5]

Creole style is inspired by classic European cuisine whereas Cajun stems from a more rustic tradition, but both adapted to the abundance of ingredients that the new continent offered, barbecuing, grilling and smoking offal and adapting dishes such as oxtail soup by adding spices and a sweet tomato base.

However, the surplus of livestock in America in the late nineteenth century meant that cheaper prime-cut meat became available to all. Jack Ubaldi's *Meat Book* (1991) describes how America became 'a nation of muscle-meat eaters [that] could afford to throw out the innards and other exotica'. Offal could be set aside, particularly as it was associated with hard times.

Australian Aboriginals are reputed to have sought out offal to find essential fats in the intestines of marsupials and emus, and the highly saturated fat from the possum, which was eaten raw.[6] In the lush coastal areas the organs of a large seagoing mammal, the dugong, were another fat source.[7] Today Australia produces large quantities of offal as byproduct of its vast meat industry, yet the majority – apart from what is used in their meat pies, which are legally permitted to contain blood vessels, snouts, tongue roots and tendons – is exported to Asia, with beef diaphragms being shipped to Japan and sheep's eyes to China.

As late as the 1970s offal was still being widely enjoyed in Australia, and so it is only recently that the stigma of its 'hoogoo' or *haut gout* (high taste) has been felt. Some explain this reticence as a desire to assert national identity, and to separate from recent waves of Asian immigration. Offal eating becomes marginalized, eaten by the rest of the population only in 'ethnic' restaurants; then, in a cycle mimicking the European and American experience, it is gradually taken up by fashionable society as a new and exciting culinary possibility.

Some avoid *andouillettes* because of their scent of excrement; others prize this dish of coarsely chopped pig offal encased in small intestine or colon, forming sausages served hot or cold, and originating from eastern and northern France.

However, in New Zealand, though Maori consumption of bush offal may have greatly reduced, in the country as a whole, which has relatively less immigration than in Australia, European offal staples have retained their nostalgic hold.

In the West we tend to think of France as the heart of refined haute cuisine. From the time of Charlemagne (*c.* 742–814), where meat was available it would have been roasted on a spit, often with offal parts skewered along with carcass meat. The poor were more likely to use offal to add flavour to cereals and vegetable soups. This food of the poor was sold on the street, and its vendors, or *restaurers*, gave their name to the first soup shops, or restaurants, in sixteenth-century Paris. Pig offal sausages, *andouilles*, and the smaller ones known as *andouillettes*, are made from coarsely chopped tripe, pork parts and chitterlings, and are recorded by Alexandre Dumas in his culinary dictionary of 1873. *The Ladies' New Book of Cookery*,

The herbivore dugong, sometimes known as the sea cow, prized for its high-protein fat by Australian Aboriginals. In India its oil was thought to be an aphrodisiac.

published in 1852 in New York, recognizes both the culinary authority of French cuisine and its ability to use all parts of an animal:

> It is generally admitted that the French excel in the economy of their cooking. By studying the appropriate flavours of every dish, they contrive to dress all the broken pieces of meats.[8]

Offal permeates everyday meat dishes in France: *pot-au-feu*, into which all parts might go; *coq au vin*, thickened with

Tripe stew from Normandy, enriched with calf or ox foot and suet. Every year the society La Triperie d'Or holds a competition to find the best maker of *tripes à la mode de Caen*.

the chicken's own blood, which some say was first eaten by Julius Caesar; *alicot*, a mishmash of poultry bits, giblets, head, feet and wing tips from the Languedoc, cooked in goose fat then casseroled with vegetables in stock; *boeuf à la mode*, a fifteenth-century dish in which beef is lardoned with strips of fat pork skin and stewed in a liquor thickened with calf's foot; calf's liver in all manner of ways; sheep's kidneys cooked in wine, perhaps with juniper berries, and served on toast; calf's head in a vinaigrette; calf's feet cooked in white wine *à la menagère* (for the thrifty housewife); brains with black butter; sweetbreads, *ris de veau, ris d'agneau*; ox tongue stewed with butter, mushrooms and mustard and so on, through its tripes and offal stocks, until we reach all the pâtés of France with goose foie gras to the fore. In Nice and Marseille *pieds et pacquets* are lamb trotters and tripe stuffed with salt pork and cooked slowly in a wine and tomato sauce, though nowadays trotters are sometimes omitted from the dish.

Though French gastronomy draws on traditional cooking, it is often perceived as aristocratic, invested with a sense of opulence and technical expertise. Taillevent (1310–1395), chef to French royalty in the fourteenth century, draws on an abundance of offal parts in his recipes in *Le Viandier*, a book of medieval courtly cuisine. Harking back to *Apicius* and classical Roman food, he takes an interest in whether dishes are healthy or not. From the nineteenth century on French cooking showed an increasing tendency to disguise offal.

A great chef of the early nineteenth century, Antonin Carême – who cooked for the diplomat and gourmet Talleyrand, Louis XVIII, Napoleon, Tsar Alexander I, the Prince Regent to the English throne and the financier James Mayer de Rothschild – brought a sense of grandeur to cooking. In the Russian manner, he served one dish at a time rather than all together (*service à la Russe*); in consequence a particular offal part could be savoured in its own right. He was against using offal innards and parts such as cockscombs as mere garnishes in the Renaissance manner, though he was responsible for the development of classic sauces that were often invested with offal. The French chef Auguste Escoffier (1846–1935) did not approve of sauces that masked the flavour of the basic ingredients of a dish. His *sole à la Normande* was a subtle play of fish, truffles and herbs: 'And now the veiling sauce . . . must have calf's kidney and salt pork for foundation.'[9]

Alexander Dumas includes in his *Dictionary of Cuisine* an anecdote in which Charles VII, after fighting the English, feasts on a plate of pigs' trotters, the soft gelatinous meat coated with breadcrumbs. The dish was assembled by women in the town of St Ménehould, hence *à la Sainte Menehould.* Another recipe, for turkey giblets with turnips, appears to be traditional offal fare, yet the preparation and presentation suggest a move away from peasant food. Since the latter part of the twentieth century there has been a tendency in France to eat less offal, given its sometimes high calorie and cholesterol content.

The regional variations in French cuisine have survived to some extent, based on what ingredients are available and on local culture. Thus areas which border Germany and have been historically strongly contested tend to favour German gastronomy, with robust dishes like blood-pudding soup. In Alsace-Lorraine, despite its highly productive agricultural land, German settlers from less fertile lands brought with them a frugality that has continued to affect the food culture, and has fostered the use of offal.[10]

A few years ago in France, November was designated the official month of offal (*le mois des abats*) across the country.

A soup with liver dumplings made from ground beef liver, breadcrumbs, onion and garlic make a warming Austrian comfort food.

There has been an association for lovers of andouillette sausages, Association Amicale des Amateurs d'Andouillette Authentique, since the 1970s. Yet such tastes seem to be increasingly for the minority, or survive because they satisfy foreign tourists' idea of French cuisine.

In Austria and Germany there is a tradition of meaty offal-infused broths and soups, liver dumplings, offal force-meat stuffed in ravioli or encased in pancakes, and more simply slices of calf's liver with onion and herbs in the Tyrol, calf's tongue seasoned with crushed anchovies and lemon, and sautéed kidneys cooked in lard. The traditions of south-ern Bavarian cooking include lung stew. Liver dumplings are popular across central Europe, the most renowned being *Leberknödel*.[11] *Kronfleischküche* is a beef-offal-rich soup or stew of veal liver, tongue, sweetbreads and heart, and there are many traditional dishes made from udder. A type of goulash that uses venison heart is known as *Hirschgulasch*, and *Markkloesschen* are dumplings made with beef bone marrow, which are traditionally added to *Hochzeitssuppe*, or wedding soup, in some regions. *Blutwurst*, or blood sausage, is still widely eaten today, but mainly by the older generation, and finds a parallel with Polish *kaszanka* sausage, Belgian and French *boudins* and English black pudding.

The political history of the Jews has led to a cuisine that combines Russian, North African, Polish, Spanish, Romanian, Austrian, Middle Eastern and German tastes and more. The Sephardic Jewish tradition tends towards highly spiced, lightly cooked offal with a particular fondness for brain, whereas Ashkenazi dishes are more slowly cooked and simply seasoned; they include all types of offal, but especially liver, sweetbreads and tongue.[12] Sephardis have a long history of eating lamb and its offal, known as Ashkenazi beef. This is rustic fare, often springing from economic hardship: dishes include offal stuffed into mutton tripes and tied with string to enrich a thin broth. This might then be used again and again when times were hard.

The influence of the Romans on Jewish cuisine can be found in a preference for udder, now mainly seen as peasant food, but until the early twentieth century highly prized, roasted or stewed, and reserved for special occasions.[13] Spleen – made into German *Miltzwurst*, a spleen sausage – and lungs are an important part of this cuisine, such as veal lungs in Viennese *Kalbsbeuschel*. Pickled herring milt or roes, the long pale organs filled with seminal matter, are a delicacy. Guided by dietary proscriptions, poultry offal dominates, with chopped chicken liver one of the mainstays of festive appetizers or *forspeis*. The German poet Hans Wilhelm Kirchof, in 1562, comments on the ability of the Jews to rear goose and their taste for its liver.[14] In the second decade of the twentieth century, James Joyce invests the Jewish protagonist of *Ulysses* (1922) with a love of offal:

Mr Leopold Bloom ate with relish the inner organs of beasts and fowls. He liked thick giblet soup, nutty gizzards, a stuffed roast heart, liverslices fried with crust-crumbs, fried hencods' roes. Most of all he liked grilled mutton kidneys which gave to his palate a fine tang of faintly scented urine.

Lately offal has become less sought-after in more affluent Jewish communities, certainly in America, though Israel maintains the tradition with contemporary dishes such as *me'orav yerushalmi* (Jerusalem mixed grill) with chopped chicken gizzards and offal parts.

The Normans introduced greater sophistication to the British diet, of a standard not seen since the Romans 800 years before.[15] A typical royal first course was pig or calf brawn served with mustard and fashioned into elaborate shapes, such as castles with battlements and keeps, and often accompanied by baked fruit, reminding one of the Piedmontese *il gran bollito misto*, which combines meats, including tongue, with candied fruits. In King John's time a dish of chicken might have been made with newly available spices in a black sauce thickened with liver. *The Good Housewives' Closet*, published in 1591, includes forcemeat made with liver and giblet stock. Henry v's court food contained marrow in both savoury and sweet dishes, one recipe involving a beef marrow-stuffed steak rolled up like a pancake and sweetened with honey.

In medieval times deer offal had become so little valued by some noblemen that at the end of a hunt the innards would be cast aside for their servants. Such parts were known as 'umbles', and so came about the expression 'to eat humble pie', meaning to behave or be forced to behave humbly or to apologize. This connotation contributes to a sometime sense of shame in enjoying offal, though the poor continued to eat

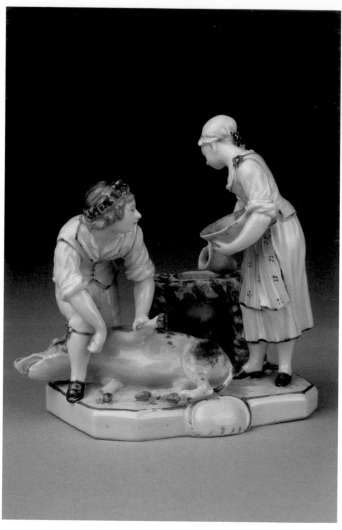

Butchering a Boar, Ludwigsburg porcelain figure, *c.* 1765. The woman is holding a bowl for the smaller parts and a jug to collect the blood to pour into the copper furnace beside her, for making blood pudding.

it. In 1826 William Cobbett, discussing some fine oxen on his journey through the British countryside, decried the fashionable spa town Cheltenham for its pimps and charlatans 'who, if suffered to live at all, ought to partake of nothing but the offal, and ought to come but one cut before the dogs and cats!'[16] They should have to eat offal because it was for the lowest of the low. Cobbett also expressed anger over landowners who had appropriated the meat of 3,000 hogs in Mullinavat, Ireland, without leaving any for the farm workers who had reared them: 'the far greater part of those who had bred and fatted these hogs were never to taste one morsel of them, no *not even* the offal.'[17]

The diarist Samuel Pepys valued tripe and haslet, or hog's entrails, above all meats, even though they brought on his gout. Rabelais (*c.* 1483–1553), though treating it as something to be avoided, nevertheless lends tripe a certain potency in describing it as so indigestible that only after feasting on *godebillios* (ox tripe) would his monster creation Gargamelle be capable of giving birth to his Gargantua. Fergus Henderson recently suggested that 'tripe stirs fear in people'.[18] Pepys, however, was an enthusiast, recording another serving of his favourite meal in his diary on 24 October 1662:

> So home and dined there with my wife upon a most excellent dish of tripes of my own directing, covered with mustard, as I have hereto seen them done at my Lord Crew's, of which I made a very great meal.

Here we encounter Pepys as the middle-class man of letters, aspiring to the aristocratic table. His appetites feed his social ambition.

Mrs Beeton, in the second half of the nineteenth century, includes a large number of offal dishes with descriptions of

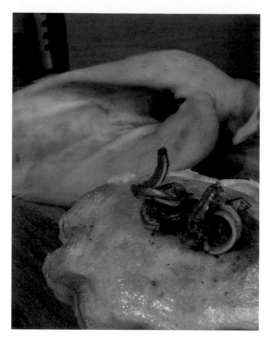

Pig's ear and pork chop pie. A pig's ear must be simmered for at least an hour until the meat, skin and cartilage become soft and palatable.

how each part should be chosen, warning against anything but young calf sweetbreads, for example, before they shrink and toughen. Sometimes she employs euphemisms: faggots are variously described as goose or savoury duck. She comments that lungs 'though edible are usually set aside for consumption by domestic pets', and that tripe and cow-heel are no longer fashionable: 'Pig's feet or pettitoes are a delicacy but it is perhaps now considered indelicate to eat them; the only method is with the teeth and fingers.'[19]

The question of delicacy or otherwise became a vital factor in class distinctions. Pepys might ape the aristocracy by gorging himself on hearty dishes of offal, but someone who aspired to be middle-class may well have felt the need to separate themselves from working- and often also from upper-class choices. Such class values have been absorbed by many cultures today, and it is in the detail of what is eaten, and by whom, that status shows its teeth.

Today the English may look to Ireland, Scotland and Wales rather than to home-grown offal credentials. The British may claim that the French and Italians are more enthusiastic about offal, although French chefs have been heard to talk of the British as if – though they cannot cook – they regularly stir up boiled tripe and onions, portions of haggis in sporrans north of the border, gristly faggots and, further south, plump fat backsides with black pudding fry-ups and steak and kidney puddings. However, when Escoffier was working at the Carlton Hotel in London during the First World War, his menus, though elegantly in French, make little mention of offal ingredients, unlike recipes written during

Steak and kidney pudding. This traditional British dish is made with beef and lamb's or pig's kidneys and steamed within suet pastry for several hours. Some recipes suggest making a small hole in the top just before serving and pouring in further gravy.

his work in France. Provisions were scarce and offal was one of the few meats that did not require coupons, so one can assume it was an hidden ingredient.

The period following the Second World War underpins many of the modern British attitudes to food. Significantly offal was not subject to rationing and provided badly needed vitamins and protein, but food writers at the time demonstrate that French terminology made these available cuts seem more appealing. Offal parts were grilled *au gratin*, and tripe was made acceptable by being presented '*Mornay*'.[20]

Is offal eaten as part of everyday fare today, even among the affluent classes? In a blog for Waitrose, arguably the most upmarket supermarket in southern Britain and a cathedral to the modern foodie, where one might expect to find the new offal-eaters, most customers interested enough to fill in an online questionnaire specified offal as the food they liked the least. The few who claimed it was their favourite – all of whom appeared to be male – wrote with an air of naughty bravado. The supermarket recently introduced a new offal-based line of 'Forgotten Cuts', but it has not sold well.

Has offal fared better in southern Europe, as it has to some extent in the southern states of America? There have long been examples of curious snobbery surrounding offal. Marco Polo, who despite his Venetian palate was well used to a panoply of rustic dishes, nonetheless denigrated Chinese peasants from the city of Kin-sai: 'As to people of the lower classes, they do not scruple to eat every kind of flesh, however unclean, without any discrimination.'[21] In Italy and Spain offal may have fallen out of favour among the younger generation, but they each have a long tradition of its consumption. Eight out of nineteen of the illuminations of the butchery trade in the medieval *Tacuinum Sanitatis* manuscripts of the Cerruti family of Verona show the purchase and domestic

Osso buco is made with beef or veal knuckle, gently stewed until the marrow is tender and the meat is about to fall from the bone.

preparation of internal organs, feet and heads. Testaccio, the district of Rome which housed its slaughterhouses into the 1970s, divided carcasses into quarters, the prime cuts going to the aristocracy, the second in line to the clergy, the third to the middle classes, the fourth to the military – and all that was left, the *quinto quarto* or 'fifth quarter', was the offal.

Offal does make up approximately a quarter of the weight of a carcass, but all the same, the idea of a *fifth* quarter, something that strictly does not make sense, hints at its uncertain status. Testaccio is still known for its long-established restaurants that serve *quinto quarto* specialities such as *coda*, or tail, stews and ragu, *zina*, or cow teats, and *milza*, or spleen. Boiled or stewed tripe is still eaten widely in Italy. Pasta sauces are enriched with ground organs like *maccanini ciociari*, angel's hair with chicken giblets and pecorino cheese, and there are many dishes of calf's liver; grills such as *fritto misto* with slices of chicken liver; *nervitt*, or calf's feet boned and flavoured with capers; and melt-in-the-mouth *osso buco*. Boiled or fried brains are again cooked in a tomato sauce, or fried up with liver and sweetbreads in *fritto misto*. The ancient Roman *pajata* or *pagliata* is the small part of lamb and veal intestines, after the *paja*, or grass, left undigested there. The unweaned calves are killed just after feeding so that the milk left inside their intestines when cooked acts with the rennet present to become a sort of soft cheese, and is usually served with *rigatoni*. Son-of-a-bitch stew, made from anything available on the American settlers' trail, relied on the same 'marrow-gut' for its distinctive flavour. *Spaghetti carbonara* was traditionally made with *guanciale*, or cured pig's cheeks, though increasingly the less fatty pancetta is used. Similarly *coratello*, the odds and ends from inside a sheep, should contain not only liver, kidneys and heart, but also lungs and other matter, though these tend to be left out today.

Southern Italian spleen sandwiches, or *pani ca meusa*, found their way to New York as *vastedda*. Cow tripe, or *callos*, is traditional in Madrid, where *callos a la madrileña* is a popular tapas dish, and across Spain liver, heart, kidneys with sherry, brains, bull's testicles (or *criadillas*) and tongue are typical. Portugal produces a variant on black pudding, cooked with flour, called *farinhato*. In one Portuguese tradition residents of Oporto disparaged those of Lisbon as lettuce-eaters (*alfacinhas*); they returned the compliment, calling the Oporto people tripe-eaters (*tripeiros*). The latter term originated in the fifteenth century, when sailors would be given all the prime cuts of meat to sustain them on their voyages, and the inhabitants of the port would be left with the remaining offal alone.

As in France, the Italian regions have their own speciality dishes, such as *zampone* (great paw) in Emilia-Romagna, a

In this beef tripe stew the deep crenulations of the honeycomb, from the reticulum chamber of a cow's stomach, trap the rich tomato liquor.

sausage made from a boned pig's trotter stuffed with pork offal. In Florence an offal speciality is *lampredotto*, with tripe from the fourth stomach of the cow, cooked in a broth containing onion, celery, carrot and tomato, and often sold on the streets from a *trippaio*, served in a bread roll with *salsa verde*. In Milan tripe is cut into thin strips and cooked for a long time to tenderize for hearty *busecca* soup.

As in medieval England, where bone marrow tended to be used in sweet dishes, in Italy pork blood enriches a chocolate dessert, *sanguinaccio*, made with cinnamon and pine nuts.

Throughout Scandinavia there are fish soups, stocks, offal-enriched fish dishes, terrines of calf, pork and veal organs. Denmark pickles many offal parts, used to enrich pork and veal dishes and for *sylte*, a pig's head dish. Finland has sheep's head, *smalahove*, served with cabbage and potatoes as a Christmas treat. The smorgasbord, a traditional Swedish buffet that is also enjoyed in Norway, Denmark and Finland,

Whale blubber is a traditional Inuit food, full of vitamin D and omega-3 fatty acids. It has a similar flavour to arrowroot biscuits and in Iceland it is pickled in whey.

includes fish offal, blood sausage, brawn and offal in sheep or pig's stomach, a dish claimed to be the forerunner of haggis.

In Iceland the scarcity of both spices for flavour and of salt for food preservation has led to the use of smoking, drying, pickling and fermenting techniques. Some traditional foods now tend only to be eaten during the ancient winter festival of Þorrablót.[22] The dishes can be challenging, such as fresh or whey-preserved sheep's head cut in half lengthwise, called *svið*.[23] When it was produced locally, whey varied in taste, but today it is more often a homogeneous product that can make many traditional foods taste the same. In *svið* the brains are removed and the hair singed away before boiling, giving the meat its distinctive smoky flavour. Sheep's head brawn, *svithasulta*, is made from all parts of the head including eyes, ears and tongue, set in its own liquor, pressed and compressed. To some extent it survives as an everyday item in Icelandic supermarkets. Whale blubber is an important element at such feasts, served pickled in whey, and has an unusual texture, 'one side . . . stringy and tough, then the texture changes gradually, and the other side becomes so soft it can be cut with a fork'.[24] *Lundabaggar* is made from internal lamb organs formed into a sausage shape, wrapped in intestine and suet and preserved in whey, and can be served roasted or smoked. Ram's and lamb's testicles are also preserved in whey. On Melrakkaslétta soured lambs' trotters and trotters' brawn are eaten. *Magall* is pressed sheep's stomach, smoked and served in slices. Sheep's blood pudding, *blóðmör*, and liver sausage, *lifrarpylsa*, are staples of such feasts, served cold and in slices.

British blood pudding and haggis are similar to *blóðmör* and *lifrarpylsa*, but are spiced and have a coarser texture. They

Lamb's testicles, lamb's headcheese, blood and liver pudding, along with rolled lamb and lamb's breast, all preserved in sour milk whey. *Súrmatur* is a traditional Icelandic food and is also made from whale meat.

Icelandic boiled lamb's head or *svið*.

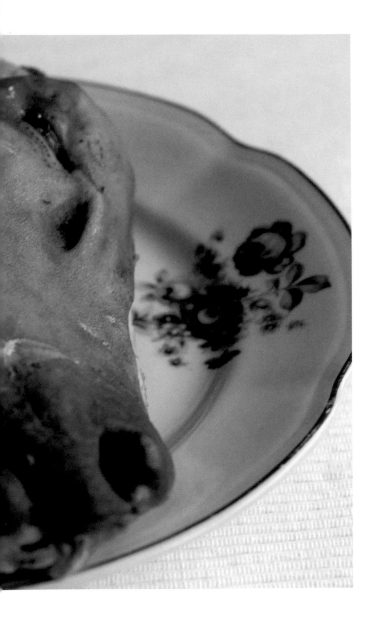

remain popular ingredients in the Black Country in particular, and in Scotland, where both are available in some chip shops, fried in batter. The Scottish have seared sheep's head, or *heid*, and a sheep's head broth known as *powsowdie*, sometimes made with feet and neck of mutton and stewed with barley, dried peas, carrot, turnip, leeks and parsley. Both are national dishes, though they have fallen out of favour. A pig's head brawn, known as potted *heid*, is markedly similar to its Scandinavian counterparts.

Singed sheep's head is one of the traditional dishes of the Buriats, a nomadic people now settled in southern Siberia around Lake Baikal. Their cuisine also includes raw liver and boiled stomach pudding.[25] Traditionally, in a diet relatively low in carbohydrates and high in fat and animal protein, Inuit hunters are said to consider the liver, cut from the seal carcass and eaten when still warm, the most prized part of a kill. Inuits might offer anyone suffering from shock a slice of raw liver, chiselled from a frozen store. *Muktuk* is a dish of frozen whale skin and blubber.

Given the cheapness of offal compared with other cuts of meat, there is sense in increasing the appetite for offal, but it remains not just a conceptual but a technical challenge. The American chef Thomas Keller writes:

> It's easy to cook a *filet mignon*, or to sauté a piece of trout . . . and call yourself a chef. But that's not real cooking. That's heating. Preparing tripe, however, is a transcendental act.[26]

Offal can be difficult to prepare well, and attitudes to offal are ambiguous. Inuit traditional practice may seem primitive or authentic. American food writers may suggest that Europe is relatively without prejudice. We buy new offal recipe books in the West, and find them challenging, even exciting, but when it comes to buying and eating offal many are hesitant. Much offal has to be pre-ordered, and even then, for some less commonly available body parts one has to go to 'ethnic' butchers, particularly those which have a more direct relationship with their animals' slaughter.

4
Macho Status

Gérard Depardieu is nonplussed in the film *Green Card* (dir. Peter Weir, 1990) by the very notion of a vegetarian. His character believes that, for red-blooded men at least, the consumption of meat is essential. If meat is a must, then the meatiest meat must surely be offal.[1]

There is something masculine about offal, or so we are led to believe. It is associated with the virtues of strength and virile sexuality, but also with what is physically dirty and often less morally pure. Manly men should lack that queasiness often associated with feminine sensibility. In an episode of the American television series *Rawhide* in the 1960s, a cowboy finds shelter for a woman in a freezing prairie blizzard, deep in the carcass of a newly fallen buffalo. They are kept warm within the freshly steaming entrails.

A bullfighter may consume the testicles of a slain bull to enhance his masculinity. An association with bloody offal can suggest gross brutality. The thriller *Le Boucher* (dir. Claude Chabrol, 1970) features a character named Popaul who has recently returned from the Vietnam War. A working-class butcher, his raw, primitive self is only just kept beneath the surface. He is able to articulate an instinctive violence in terms of his butchering trade:

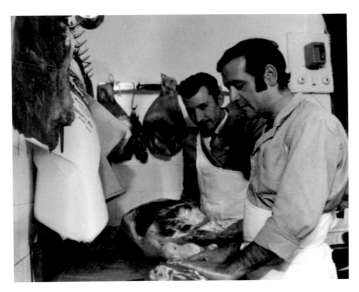

The murderous Popaul, played by Jean Yanne, at work in his butcher's shop in *Le Boucher* (dir. Claude Chabrol, 1970).

I have a lot of blood – my blood doesn't stop flowing. I know about blood. I've seen so much blood, blood flowing . . . Once when I was little, I fainted when I saw blood – they all smell the same, that of animals and that of men. Some is more red than others, but all have exactly the same smell.

It is this barely concealed violence that evokes a sexual response in a cultured, mild-mannered schoolmistress.

Although offal may have come to represent low-status food, its recent re-emergence as a fashionable if controversial choice is aligned to a characteristically masculine stance. In these times of greater equality between the sexes our gendered attitudes to offal could be said to reveal a sort of nostalgia for an obsolete stereotype of dominant masculinity.

Mixed tails, trotters and various other parts for sale, in Brixton Market, South London, on a Saturday afternoon.

Being seen to enjoy offal can undermine notions of femininity in a woman. Of course, some women find offal delicious and far from off-putting and many a man feels the reverse – yet the general tendency is borne out by any ad hoc survey of responses from men and women in the West. When women say they love offal, there can be a quality of self-conscious *brio* in their assertions, a desire to confound expectations, that confirms rather than denies this suggestion.

In J. G. Farrell's novel *The Siege of Krishnapur* (1973), set at the time of the Indian Mutiny, the British community is besieged and becomes surrounded by piles of bodies, referred to as decaying offal, that seem to represent moral as well as physical corruption. The initial cause of the Mutiny had been both Hindu and Muslim objections to sepoys being ordered to use forbidden animal grease on their rifles. Significantly a young English woman, who has earlier been ostracized

Weighing up the offal at Crawford Market in South Mumbai, 2010.

for a sexual indiscretion, becomes adept at producing makeshift cartridges to keep the insurgents at bay, but since she makes them from beeswax and rancid butter, she effectively circumvents the initial cause of the revolt. She takes a male role, the only one able to solve a practical military problem, but her status is also that of peasant, sitting 'cross-legged like a native in the bazaar'.

The photographer Eli Lotar's reportage includes a series of Parisian slaughterhouse scenes taken in 1929, the trotters lined up in the street like a queue in waiting, seeming to look forward to militarism ahead. Inside the abattoir he captures severed heads of cattle, their eyes rolling as if in appeal or from above shoots men at work in the confusion and mess of killing. The contemporary artist Victoria Reynolds paints vivid slaughterhouse images, the result of a visit to a Lapp reindeer abattoir, and reminiscent of the dolour of Rembrandt's *Slaughtered Ox* of 1655. These artists are part of a tradition that despite the flux of history suggests that this is who we are, just

A bowl of lamb's hearts.

flesh, corruptible and fragile. Gradually in the West we have withdrawn from such truths, so that the realities of slaughter and butchery are pushed aside. They seem too primitive and at best are allowed to represent masculine virility.

Butchery is a skill requiring strength and precision and a certain lack of sentimentality, both to be able to slaughter and to take on the attitudes required by such a trade. If we are seen principally in relation to our work, then to be a butcher either in the abattoir or a butcher's shop makes demands on the sensibilities that traditionally have been seen as male. The collective noun for butchers is 'a goring'. Butchery is associated with blood, on the apron, on the hands, the metallic smell in the air, the stains and rivulets on the floor and the cries of slaughter. Blood and the assumed extra bloodiness of offal suggest violent death and the field of battle.

The novelist Barbara Pym, writing in the 1950s, notices how men are assumed to require more meat than women in their diet, to comic effect. In *Jane and Prudence*, set in the post-Second World War period when meat was still scarce, Jane worries that the vicar may drop by while they are eating liver for supper. The cook, whose nephew is the local butcher, reassures her that he 'shares out the offal on a fair basis, madam, but everybody can't have it every time.'[2] P. G. Wodehouse has *Offal* as the title of a racy novel in the short story 'Bestseller' from his collection *Mulliner Nights* (1933). If offal comes into a story it is usually there for a reason. One might lazily make a character a shop assistant, a baker, an IT consultant . . . but if they are a butcher, or eat offal, then this is unlikely to be a neutral choice. Sarah Daniels's play *Gut Girls* (1988), for example, is about women who worked in the slaughter-sheds of Deptford, East London, and has them deep in entrails. It recalls Charles Dickens's account in *Oliver*

Twist of Smithfield Market, where the working conditions are 'nearly ankle-deep with filth and mire'. The women's work brought them relatively high wages and social freedom compared with those working in domestic service, but their bloody business confronts Victorian and perhaps even contemporary notions of the feminine.

Julie Powell's account of mastering the art of butchery takes place in a small upstate New York butcher's shop, where she describes herself as 'lovingly manipulating offal with gore-begrimed fingers'.[3] For a female to train as a butcher is considered unusual even today, and Powell enjoys the experience of people listening 'to a woman holding a butcher knife', but her underlying motivation – to get over an extramarital affair – somewhat undercuts any sense of empowerment. It is as if the strenuous practice in learning to wield a knife effectively, cleaving, separating sinew from interconnecting tissue, or 'seams', and the art of scraping bones, all help her to address and readjust her emotional state. Making blood sausage mixture by spooning the mixture into a mechanical stuffer, easing the pork into the intestinal casing, she slyly describes as being 'like the activity it often resembles . . . more fun with two people'. It might be argued that her pleasure in the task comes from this adoption of the male sexual role. When her training is complete she is given a set of knives engraved with the motto 'Julie Powell, *Loufoque*', French butcher's Pig Latin for 'crazy lady', affectionate but confirming her gender nonconformism.

Photographer Stephani Diani juggles with the idea of gender and conventional romantic poses in her *Offal Taste* series.[4] She photographs people in what appear to be avant-garde outfits which are made up of offal parts: a beautiful girl wears a delicate white lace top which turns out to be tripe; a male 'six-pack' torso is a string of sausages; pig's testicles are

Stephanie Diani, *Offal Taste: Snood*, 2009. These apparently formal portraits are subverted by their offal clothing, here with a medieval snood made from plaited intestine.

headphones; necklaces are oxtail segments or made up of pig's hearts; a mini skirt is a row of pig's trotters; and a grace-ful snood is made from plaited intestine. A woman sits pensively, seeming comforted by something that gently caresses her cheek: ox tongue, of course. This implicit

Stephanie Diani, *Offal Taste: Tongue*, 2009. The rawness of a beef tongue mohican plays with the idea of what should be inside being outside.

humour echoes the great sixteenth-century Giuseppe Arcimboldo with his bizarre and at the time highly fashionable portraits made up entirely of fruit, flowers, or sometimes pieces of fish and meat.

Norman Douglas's book of aphrodisiac food, *Venus in the Kitchen* (1952), offers a variety of offal dishes, though he does not elaborate exactly how fried cow's brains with herbs and spices, lamb's ears with sorrel or macaroni with finely chopped kidneys are erotic in tone or physical effect. There is about the recipes a hesitancy between self-conscious naughtiness and snobbery. Douglas quotes Aristotle as recommending sparrow's brains, *propter nimium coitum, vix tertium annum elabuntur* (on account of too much sex, they scarcely survive three years), and gives a recipe for lamb's testicles with cinnamon, cloves and saffron from Bartolomeo Scappi, personal cook to Pope Pius v. There is implicit ribaldry concerning sexual parts, such as with 'Pie of Bull's Testicles', again from Scappi, and he mentions *vulvae steriles*, a dish of sow's parts from *Apicius* praised by Horace, Pliny and Martial.

Killing a pig, particularly when it has been reared as part of the family in rural communities, can be distressing. In Thomas Hardy's *Jude the Obscure* (1895), Jude is forced to make the kill himself when a professional pigsticker fails to turn up, goaded by his more callous wife, Arabella. Just as Julie Powell's learning to butcher clarifies her feelings, so this slaughter exposes the incompatibilities in Jude and Arabella's relationship, and Jude is emasculated. Arabella insists that he try to kill the pig slowly, for 'every good butcher keeps un bleeding long', but Jude in his distress knocks over a jug of fresh blood which she had intended for 'blackpot', a type of black pudding, and she despises him for it. Jude judges himself a 'tender-hearted fool': 'Jude felt dissatisfied with himself *as a man* at what he had done' (my italics). Arabella is proud of being part of a rural tradition that wastes nothing, valuing every part of the pig. Yet she throws its penis, 'the scrap of offal', at Jude as a gross insult. The description of its 'soft cold substance' evokes an image of Jude as impotent.[5]

Chicken's feet have very much the appearance of old ladies' hands.

Given its generally beleaguered position in the West, clubs have been formed to promote interest in offal. Many of these are male-only affairs. In New York a dining club for adventurous eaters delights in sampling bizarre, 'fear factor' foods. It calls itself The Gastronauts, as if its members boldly go where no man has gone before.[6] In England a Manchester-based group of friends gets together to promote and celebrate offal, 'a much maligned food'; their aim is partly to shock, partly an opportunity to enjoy male solidarity. The language they use is deliberately raunchy, calling one meeting 'Nads and Glands', serving lamb's testicles with citrus, muscovado sugar and paprika as Mexi-cojones, joking that they could not

get any cock's tails for a prawn cocktail. Even the pudding must contain gelatine, a thickening agent derived from boiled animal hides and bones.

The restaurant critic Giles Coren has noted the tendency of fashionable restaurants to use spare, unambiguous language on their menus of late, which he designates as combining 'brevity and the vernacular' in a form of 'pretentious unpretentiousness'.[7] Yet Cay Tre, a Vietnamese restaurant in London, was reluctant to name a dish of pig's trotters 'mock dog', though dog is a popular choice in Vietnam; clearly the owner is aware of his customers' limitations. Offal eating may be contentious, but pet eating is obscene. There is a certain appropriateness about a restaurant following, say, a long tradition of Turkish grilled offal, displaying a clutch of large, raw lamb's testicles in its window, but offal clubs are reintroducing something into their diet for reasons that go beyond cultural authenticity or questions of flavour alone.

Despite our cultural complexities, many would nonetheless still associate haggis with a masculine Scottish tradition. The food historian Alan Davidson suggests that haggis derives from Roman times. A pudding made from offal and oats within a sheep's stomach or caul, haggis's precise ingredients remain mysterious, but since it is known to contain sheep's lungs, the u.s. Food Standards Agency has prohibited its import into America for the last 40 years, a decision reinforced by the fear of bse that has been present since 1989. The origins of the word are Scandinavian, derived from the Old Norse *hoggra*, or the Icelanic *haggw*, meaning to hew or strike with a sharp weapon.[8] It may also possibly stem from Old Hebrew *hagga*, meaning that which causes one to stagger. Some claim it was an easily transportable food for travelling cattle drovers, others that it was the reward to workmen-slaughterers after the laird had taken the prime cuts.

An air of comedy attaches itself to haggis. There are claims that it comes from a rare beast with a pair of short legs along one side and long on the other, ideal for tearing round Scottish mountains. A Monty Python poem relates the sad tale of a boy who ate himself: 'His liver and his lights and lung,/His ears, his neck, his chin, his tongue . . .'.[9]

Outrage broke out in the press recently when the historian Catherine Brown dared to suggest that the Scottish national dish had been enjoyed in England 200 years before.[10] Whether a recipe in *The English Hus-wife* of 1615 proves that haggis is English in origin, or merely shows that the English were keen to adopt tasty dishes from their neighbours, it is revealing that such a notion was seen as undermining Scottish sovereignty. Alexander McCall Smith defended his birthright in the *New York Times* in mock-macho horror, recommending that visitors to his country try some haggis and wash it down with a thimble of whisky 'to neutralize the taste'.[11]

Robert Burns's famous 'Address to a Haggis' (1786) has Scotland as female and haggis as brave male warrior:

> Fair fa' your honest, sonsie face,
> Great chieftain o the puddin'-race!
>
> Auld Scotland wants nae skinking ware
> That jaups in luggies:
> But, if ye wish her gratefu' prayer,
> Gie her a Haggis!

I have implied that offal is an expression of rugged masculinity, yet some of the greatest chefs, while happily incorporating offal into their menus, have disguised and thus made light of its potential effect. Carême would disguise one dish as another, delighting in intricate and ostentatious presentation a world apart from a desire to show offal as straight from a beast's insides or extremities. The experience of the French Revolution may have encouraged him to develop elegant techniques to distance himself from what might have reminded him of its barbarities, but its effect was both to camouflage and feminize, gaining for offal a hybrid status and access to the tables of those in power.

A character in Petronius's *Satyricon* prepares a feast that is entirely made from every part of the pig, but dressed up as other foods. Perhaps the idea of hiding offal in prepared food is not always a matter of shame: the disguise itself may be pleasing to us, one thing presented as another, like a moment of food theatre. We may think we want to know

Kate Lynch, *The Runner in the Slaughterhouse*, 2007, oil on canvas.

Elina eating a sheep's eye, Cyprus, 2012. The head is the most pungent in both smell and taste and considered the greatest delicacy. Children are often given the brains as the easiest parts to eat.

what we are eating, macho guts and all, but in practice we often do not.

The chef Heston Blumenthal enjoys such illusions and in his BBC television programme *Heston's Feasts* (2010) he chose a fairy-tale theme to make a pig's head out of pig offal. Cock's testicles were coated and coloured to present them as magic Jack and the Beanstalk beans, which his diners could then find charming rather than alarming. Blumenthal undercuts any expectation of real offal by presenting it as a fictional huntsman's kill from the story of Snow White, each part becoming 'sexy', though one might argue that a testicle un-adulterated is quite sexy enough. Presenting real as pretend offal in a fanciful feminized setting is a means of allowing the different pork body parts to be tasted without prejudice, in all their variety.

However, one actual pig part that was not included was the eyeball. Seen as a succulent delicacy in many cultures from Sudan to Iceland, Blumenthal was forced to admit that he simply could not bring himself to eat one, and made a substitute instead. We see him try to eat an eyeball, but he finds it impossible, seemingly amazed to have found something he is not able to sample without prejudice, appalled at himself for such a 'knee jerk reaction I couldn't control'. The apparently macho chef allows us to see him caught out for once in a very modern distaste.

5
As Ritual

If you purchase a chicken, you may still come across a small package inside that contains the liver, heart, kidneys and neck, all swimming in a pool of blood. These are for making gravy or stock but also confirm a bird's former life. They have the look of a talisman, a bag of tricks for telling fortunes, a magical scapular of uncertain significance.

Since the Old English root of 'to bless' comes from *blœd-sian*, meaning to sprinkle with sacrificial blood, one might claim that offal is the most blessed of meats, and so blessed are the offal eaters. But what is blessed can seem cursed. We are carnivores in part, asserting our supremacy over the animal world, but this fact also confirms our animal selves. When an animal was sacrificed to the gods in ancient Greece, the entrails, and particularly the liver, would be excised immediately after slaughter and examined to judge whether it was acceptable to the gods. While the muscle meat would be cooked and shared out, the offal would be retained by the priests and cook-sacrificer. In Roman culture the internal organs, or *exta*, of a sacrifice might foretell the future.[1]

It is no wonder that superstitious beliefs have grown up around offal, so associated is it with our thoughts and feelings. In Harar, in eastern Ethiopia, one can still see an ancient open-air ritual in which men wrap offal around sticks, which are then held in their mouths for wild hyenas to snatch. Since hyenas have one of the strongest bites of all animals, the hyena-men earn money through this display of risk and primordial chutzpah. In Liberia a traditional belief holds that strength may be gained from eating the heart of a child; the former rebel leader Milton Blahyi admitted to taking part in such ritual practice during the civil war of 1979–93.[2]

The medieval English punishment for a man who committed high treason was to be hanged, drawn and quartered. This involved castrating and disembowelling the subject while they were still conscious, forcing them to observe their organs being burnt before their eyes. Such executions were practised in other European countries with some variations: the viscera were sometimes placed in the victim's mouth, as if he were consuming his own substance. This finds a nightmarish parallel in an account of the Srebrenića massacre of 1995; the International Criminal Tribunal Judge Fouad Riad reported that a man had been 'skewered to a tree and made to eat the innards of his grandson'.[3]

There is something about the internal organs, and particularly the heart and blood, that seems to represent the individual. In the Roman Catholic Church transubstantiation is believed to convert the bread and wine used in the sacrament of the Eucharist into the body and blood of Christ, so that the priest and communicants believe they are consuming actual flesh and blood. Miracles are sometimes attributed to saints' bodily parts, the most powerful relics being from saints that had come into direct bodily contact with Christ.

Catholics, Anglo-Catholics and Lutherans honour the idea of the Sacred Heart of Jesus, which is typically represented by an image of the Christ-child or adult Jesus with a flaming heart pierced by a lance, as at the Crucifixion. A cult

Harry Clarke, *Apparition of the Sacred Heart* window, designed 1918, clear, coloured and flashed glass. The exposed and bleeding heart represents the idea of Christ's love and mercy, and also his martyrdom.

grew up around this notion in the sixteenth century, and the Sacred Heart image is still common on medals and scapulars, stuck to a small square of blood-red flannel.

Blood, or the idea of blood, can be imbued with magical powers. In Judaism, following Old Testament law, blood should be drained from animal and bird meat, while the Philippine *Iglesia ni Cristo* prohibits the eating of *dinuguan* because this popular stew is made with pork blood: 'For the life of a creature is in the blood, and I have given it to you to make atonement for yourselves on the altar; it is the blood that makes atonement for one's life' (Leviticus 17:11). Thus blood and the wounded heart of God made man stands for human culpability. In the Old Testament the destruction of offal can extinguish sin: 'the fat, and the kidneys, and the caul above the liver of the sin offering, he burnt upon the altar; as the Lord commanded Moses' (Leviticus 9:10).

In some branches of Judaism it is permitted and even encouraged to donate organs to save another's life. Jehovah's Witnesses, on the other hand, will only allow organ and tissue transplants if all the blood has first been removed, since they do not permit blood transfusions. Their position brings to mind Shylock's dilemma in *The Merchant of Venice* when, about to cut away Antonio's flesh according to their contract, he is warned by Portia: 'This bond doth give thee here no jot of blood; The words expressly are a pound of flesh' (IV, I). Since blood is an integral part of flesh, arguably Shylock does not receive justice, flesh being of its nature bloody.

Japanese Shintoism considers the body, once dead, to be unclean, so it can be problematic to harvest organs. This is also thought to injure the connection between a dead person and those they leave behind, termed the *itai*. Romany gypsies also resist organ donation, believing that the body should remain whole so that the soul may retrace its steps a year after death.

One story that occurs in many versions in European and Far Eastern folklore is 'The Legend of the Eaten Heart', in which an unfaithful wife is usually served the heart of her lover by a vengeful husband. In one of the stories of *The Decameron*, Tancredi kills his daughter's lover Guiscardo and sends her the heart in a golden cup. She adds poison to it, drinks it and dies, clutching his heart to her own. In another tale Guillaume de Roussillon murders his wife's lover and gives her the heart to eat, disguised in a dish of boar. When Roussillon reveals his deception, she throws herself from a high tower. These stories establish the heart as the seat of the emotions, and of love in particular. The murderers attempt to dishonour their victims, but their actions effectively unite the lovers in both a physical and spiritual sense.

This theme of unwitting and enforced cannibalism is popular in horror films as well as sadomasochistic and thriller literature. Real-life serial killers, too, have been known to store and eat the offal of their victims. The American Ed Gein, arrested in 1957 on suspicion of multiple murders, kept organs in his fridge and many other macabre keepsakes about the house, such as chair seats fashioned from human skin and a shoe box containing nine vulvas. He is said to have inspired the Jame Gumb ('Buffalo Bill') serial killer in Thomas Harris's *The Silence of the Lambs* (1988), with his bodysuit made of human skin. The elegant cannibalistic tendencies of the character Hannibal Lecter are perhaps better remembered; he describes himself as 'having an old friend for lunch' meaning enjoying eating human liver 'with some fava beans and a nice Chianti'. Armin Meiwes, known as Der Metzgermeister (the Master Butcher), was tried in 2003 for the murder of one Bernd Jürgen Brandes, whom he had cannibalized. His defence was that Brandes had been a willing accomplice and that they had together attempted to eat the latter's penis. It had proved too tough when raw, and Meiwes had subsequently sautéed it in wine and garlic. The case inspired a host of films and songs, such as the Marilyn Manson album *Eat Me, Drink Me* (2007).

There are many mythological beliefs concerning offal. Claude Lévi-Strauss examines the myths of the Bororo Indians of central Brazil and their beliefs about the origins of the distant Pleiades stars.[4] A murdered man's ghost demands to be properly buried and have his entrails scattered, and these floating viscera become the stars. Guianian myth juxtaposes two stories, so that when the murdered man's entrails become the stars, the river teems with fish. An Arecuna myth links the aquatic and celestial with the tale of an old woman who is discovered to have been secretly feeding her son-in-law with fish from her own uterus. Stones that slice and kill the woman fall into the river and are transformed into flesh-eating piranhas. Her liver floats to the surface and becomes *mureru brava*, an aquatic plant, whose seeds are said to be the woman's heart. The North American Zuni believe that stars spring from the lungs of a dismembered ogre, whereas Navajo mythology holds that aquatic animals are born from the submerged entrails of a huge bear.

Cannibal practices can be a practical business when human flesh is the only available source of nourishment in times of war or famine. Eating the organs of a vanquished enemy might also be seen as a way of gaining spiritual as well as physical ascendancy.

James Bradley's non-fiction book *Flyboys* (2003) details an incident of captured American airmen being harvested for food on Chichi-jima island, Japan, during the Second World War. What is of interest here is the culinary attention given to human offal. The Japanese soldiers were intensely curious about the removal of body parts, suggesting an aspect of ritual towards the enemy, and perhaps a degree of objectivity. Choice offal parts were kept for senior officers:

> That night Major Matoba and a number of other army officers brought a delicacy to Admiral Kinzio Mori's headquarters. Matoba had had Floyd (Hall)'s liver prepared specially for the party. 'I had it pierced with bamboo sticks and cooked with soya sauce and vegetables,' Matoba said. 'The meat was cut in very small pieces and pierced together by bamboo shoots.'

As is often the case in Japanese cuisine, there is an emphasis on the health-giving properties of the food:

> 'The officers remarked how liver was good for the stomach' . . . Matoba remembered: 'Admiral Mori mentioned that during the Chinese-Japanese war human liver was

Vikramaditya Cooked for Kali, c. 1800, pigment on paper. The goddess Kali and her entourage of ghosts have tied up the folklore hero and are about to boil him alive.

eaten as a medicine by the Japanese troops. All the other officers agreed that liver was good medicine for the stomach.'[5]

The bloodsucking vampire figure appears in many cultures' occult beliefs across the globe, including Eastern Europe, African voodoo and Asian folklore. The Betsileo people of Madagascar are said to hanker not only for the blood but for the nail clippings of the nobility. Ancient beliefs about vampires are also rife in South America.

Vampire figures have gradually become less alarming and more conventionally appealing, and their bloodsucking seems more seductive than threatening. For evidence of this one only has to compare the diseased, seething Count Orlok played by Max Schreck in the F. W. Murnau film *Nosferatu* (1922) with recent posters depicting the characters of the *Twilight* series of films: serious, but young, clean-cut and uniformly attractive, with only a hint of elongated incisor.

In China snake-blood wine is a traditional stimulant, brewed from the living heart of a freshly butchered snake. This idea that a still-living organ has greater potency for the consumer is borne out by stories of rich foreigners who seek out live monkey brains to renew their potency. The monkey is reputedly trapped beneath a table with its head held in a central hole, the better to spoon out its brains. Hunters of the Masai tribe of East Africa traditionally sustained themselves on long treks by drinking milk mixed with freshly tapped blood from their cattle, just as ancient Egyptians, in times of drought, gained essential extra protein in a similiar manner.[6] Nowadays the Masai drink fresh blood only at ritual events, though it is still given as a nourishing drink to the ill and infirm.

In Inuit culture seal blood is thought to strengthen human blood. After slaughter hunters divide and eat the seal liver, then drink the blood in a shared cup, taking pieces of brain and fat together with the muscle meat. Finally the women and children are allowed to join in the feast. This shared ritual is intended to show respect for the kill, and is comparable to Catholic transubstantiation beliefs in that the Inuit believe that thereby they incorporate the body and soul of the seal into themselves. In similar vein the Ohlone tribe, of what is presently the California Bay area, undertook a solemn ritual after the killing of a deer. After 'a prayer and gesture of thanks to the deer' the carcass was taken back to the village:

> The stomach is removed, stuffed with certain entrails and choice pieces of meat from around the kidneys, and presented to the men who accompanied the hunter. The liver is set aside for an old woman who has fed him mush and seed cakes since he was a child.[7]

Human sacrifice among the Aztecs was complex in its refined symbolism and bloody practice. Either slaves or captured enemies might be sacrificed, and it has been argued that it was considered an honour to meet death in such a way. On the night of the O' Nothing Days, a captive would be stretched out across a high altar as the evening star reached its zenith. The priest would set light to the heart, excise it and hold the organ aloft in honour of the sun god. After sacrifice, vessels of blood would be carried through the streets and the flayed pelts of the victims were worn by the exuberant warrior, even as they began to tighten and rot. Banquets held after such ceremonies served up the sacrificed flesh, heart and internal organs with contrasting decorum and culinary grace.[8]

Bodily organs are also sometimes held to affect both character and disposition. In European culture the bodily humours were thought to be affected by diet. Eating brains or heart, for example, was thought to produce melancholy. The role of the inner organs in human personality and health were also important in the school of *Unani* or *Unani-tibbi*, a system of medicine that continues to be of significance in the Islamic world, particularly in the Middle East and Central Asia.[9] This in turn was derived from Greek and Arabic learning, in particular from Galen, physician to Marcus Aurelius in the second century.

The critic Ambrose Bierce wrote of these shifting associations in his satirical *The Devil's Dictionary* (1911):

> Liver *n.* A large organ thoughtfully provided to be bilious with. The sentiments and emotions which every literary anatomist now knows to haunt the heart were believed to haunt the liver . . . It was one time considered the seat of life; hence its name – liver, the thing we live with . . . [10]

He goes on to extol the virtues of Strasbourg pâté.

Divining the future, or the will of the gods, from animal entrails (extispicy) was practised in many ancient cultures. Geology has been described as the art of divining the future by splitting open the earth and examining its innards; extispicy might have seemed just such a reliable practice in ancient Greece. Seneca's version of *Oedipus* has the blind prophet Tiresias sacrifice a bull and heifer to discover the murderer of the late king; he finds their entrails to be rotten.

In sacrifices made by Greeks and Romans before battle, a blood-red liver promised victory; if it were pale, it augured defeat. Thus when Macbeth calls his servant 'thou lily-livered boy' (v, 3), he is implying that the sickly, pale servant seems to Macbeth to prophesy defeat.

'Aztec Human Sacrifice', from the 16th-century Spanish *Codex Magliabechiano*.

In the FIFA World Cup in 2010, ancient *muti* magic was the reason for the illegal harvesting of rare South African Cape vultures.[11] Traditionally, smoking the birds' brains was thought to reveal the future, and gamblers who had bet on the results of the football matches felt this practice was worth spending the birds' black market value. In Europe of late there have been various reports of ritual killings that involve the removal of bodily organs, linked to Yoruba medicine of Nigerian derivation. Such *muti* practices can involve the removal of ears, heart and genitals, considered to be parts of special potency.

Television crime dramas, films and suspense novels provide accounts of murder investigations in which the intimate conditions of a corpse's organs reveal the cause of death. Although we may feel reassured by such apparent certainties, the aura that surrounds the postmortem and the gravitas of the pathologist or CSI investigator has come to assume much of the mystery and charisma of divination. The world-weary doctor holds aloft a slippery organ for the reverential detective to see. She uncovers the secrets of the human body: trauma, overdose, poison, strangulation, disease.

I leave it to Norman Lewis who, in describing the butchers' shops of war-torn Naples of the 1940s, captures the respect we may come to feel for offal:

> Their displays of scraps of offal are set out with art, and handled with reverence . . . chickens' heads . . . a little grey pile of chickens' intestines in a brightly polished saucer . . . a gizzard . . . calves' trotters . . . a large piece of windpipe . . . Little queues wait to be served with these delicacies.[12]

6
As Medicine

There are age-old reasons for respecting offal. The connection between food and health was developed in the second-century writings of Galen, who derived it from earlier practices. His work is based on scientific observation and experimentation, and in his theory of the balance of bodily humours. He condemns brains as phlegmatic and unwholesome, 'being both slow to pass, difficult to digest and bad, too, not least for the stomach'; but when they induce nausea, with admirable pragmatism he recommends them to be served at the end of a meal in oil, when an emetic might be required.[1] Eating spleen is too astringent, producing melancholy, while the lungs are at least easier to digest. Kidneys he particularly mistrusts, because they are wholly indigestible; belly, womb and intestines need time to digest properly. He finds liver to be the most nutritious of offal dietary aids.

Most offal is high in vitamins and minerals, and kidneys are particularly rich in zinc and iron. The heart contains taurine, which in turn is good for the heart. Tripe contains probiotics and phytonutrients, which are said to be highly nutritious. Tripe and kidneys are particularly low in calories and fat, so are suitable for the weight-conscious, though in this respect sweetbreads need to be avoided. Liver is packed with complete

Time Banishes Melancholy, Flanders, *c.* 1530, painted glass roundel. Since the time of the physician Galen, the humours, located in and about the inner organs, were thought to govern the human body. Saturn is shown here as a pig in monk's robes.

proteins and with iron, needed for haemoglobin, which transports oxygen from the lungs to the rest of the body. It also helps in the healing process and increases our resistance to infection. Yet, true to its contrary nature, offal can also be high in cholesterol, which in excess will fur up our arteries and has turned our svelte French cousins quite off this dish of kings. The effects of foie gras on the greedy gourmet are about as healthy as the forced diet of the goose.

In traditional Chinese and much Eastern medicine offal is seen – as in ancient Greek and Roman notions – as food that promotes and also sometimes challenges health and well-being. Right now there are many alternative pharmacies in the West that diagnose and prescribe not just for ethnic minorities, but increasingly for the community at large. Chinese medicine is based on a Taoist belief system wherein the perceived character of an animal is thought to imbue its body parts: snake blood, for example, is held to provide energy and cunning, and pig's feet in sweet vinegar are said to strengthen women following childbirth. Folklore more simply associates the consumption of a particular body part with the corresponding human organ: eye for an eye, womb for a womb, and so on. Hu Sihui, the fourteenth-century Chinese dietitian, advises taking boiled sheep's heart to treat heart complaints.[2] Such a theory of correspondences can also be found in the traditional Jewish diet, though the latter does not extend to the heart, brain and liver.[3]

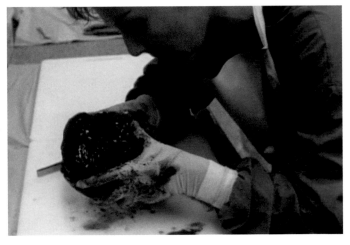

There is often a quasi-religious aspect to fictional autopsies. Here Amanda Burton playing Dr Sam Ryan in the TV series *Silent Witness*, directed by Noella Smith in 1996, reverentially examines the brain of a murder victim.

The renowned sixteenth-century gourmet physician Li Shizhen was influenced by Galen's approach in his comprehensive *materia medica*, *Bencao Gangmu*.[4] Chinese traditional medicine is essentially non-intrusive, solving health problems with gentle remedies where possible. It often involves the consumption of plants and herbs, and sometimes organ meats, as part of a prescribed dietary change. Sometimes these are in dried form, in potions or pills. Shizhen draws on concepts of the five flavours, each of which is associated with an organ of the body; the seventh-century notion of sapor, or *wu wei*, the sensation of taste; and the *qi* or 'temperature' of a food, which is said to be something more than flavour. In this context *yin* is hot, the *yang* cold. Sometimes certain food combinations need to be avoided: one should on no account eat quail meat with pig's liver, for example, for fear of getting blackheads. A stock made from rooster and asparagus, combined with the heart, lungs and liver of a black male dog, should be taken to facilitate intercourse. Shizen also investigates the effects of consuming meat from animals that have been treated poorly, and whether wild and domesticated meats have different pharmaceutical properties.

Although some handed-down simple remedies survive in the West – such as the adage warning against eating offal if suffering from depression – there is not the same holistic approach to health when treating a malady as there is in Chinese medicine. There are, of course examples of dishes that promote good health, as in a recipe for ox marrow in Gervase Markham's *The English Hus-wife* (1915), which is described as 'both good in taste and excellent sovereign for any disease, ache or flux in the veins whatsoever'.

It is possible that a tendency to see illness as something that requires the attention of a surgeon's knife has contributed to difficulties with the idea of offal. One might view the modern history of Western surgery as a craft that gradually gained ground against a more holistic approach, from the barber-surgeons of the battlefield to their elevated status today. Nonetheless, today Westerners seem increasingly open to new health strategies that have their roots in ancient folk remedies: the practice of placentophagia has enjoyed a recent comeback, associated with New Age beliefs. The consumption of the placenta is said to reduce postnatal depression while also providing nutrition for the new mother. Dr Blott of the Royal Society of Obstetricians and Gynaecologists in Britain comments that mothers are already sufficiently well-nourished in the West.[5] Some Pacific cultures bury the placenta with a sapling so that child and tree will grow up together. Indeed, the Maori word for belonging to a place is the same as that for the placenta, *tūrangawaewae*. In Korea medicine derived from placenta is a popular aid to improving the complexion; hospitals are keen to buy placentas for use in skin treatments.

Offal is often associated with germs, and there is some truth in this. The International Commission on Microbial Specifications for Foods states that 'offals often have a higher initial contamination, and are more likely to be contaminated with potential pathogens than carcass meat'.[6] Metals consumed in food tend to accumulate in animals' livers and kidneys, which mean they contain higher levels of these contaminants than other meat. Fish offal can contain cadmium and dioxins from sea and river pollution, stored in body fat and liver. The fact that offal dishes are sometimes eaten raw can also heighten the possibility of germs and parasites being passed on to the consumer. The digestive tract, for example, can harbour microorganisms such as salmonella, clostridia and E. coli. In recent years fear of bovine spongiform encephalopathy (BSE) or mad cow disease, and its association with Creutzfeldt-Jakob disease in humans, has kept beef brains out of most Western butchers' shops. Although the risks are marginal, the fear set off a strong reaction which, according to the National Federation of Meat Traders, was 'mainly due to a lack of understanding "as to what was safe and what was not" and this has never been adequately explained or understood'.[7]

The livers of most polar animals, such as polar bears, are extremely high in vitamin A. Though beneficial to the animal, this can cause life-threatening hypervitaminosis A in humans. From as early as 1596, explorers returned to Europe with tales of suffering a devastating illness, with symptoms including skin and hair loss, after eating polar bear liver. In 1912 Xavier Mertz died on an Australasian Antarctic expedition after being forced to eat husky liver in order to survive.[8] There is evidence that Inuit metabolisms have gradually become acclimatized to high levels of vitamin A.

However, some people do not feel the need to avoid dangerous foods. The Japanese delight in dodging the potential poison of *fugu* fish liver. This contains tetrodotoxin, which may induce paralysis and in some cases heart failure or suffocation. In the sixteenth century the warlord responsible for unifying Japan, Hideyoshi, banned *fugu* when some of his warriors died from consuming the delicacy.[9] However, despite further attempts to effect a ban, *fugu* has continued to be prized, even after the death in 1975 of the eminent kabuki actor Bandō Mitsugorō VIII. Only a limited number of highly trained chefs are licensed to prepare *fugu*, the flavour of which is said to be finer than that of the best foie gras. This prohibition has increased the longing for this dish. Recently non-toxic *fugu* has been successfully developed, but this has upset aesthetes and those with vested interests alike: 'When it wasn't known where fugu's poison came from, the mystery made for better conversation . . . in effect, we took the romance out of fugu.'[10] To risk death is part of the pleasure. In some regions it is nicknamed *teppou*, or gun – of the smoking variety, no doubt.

The atmosphere of danger and romance that surrounds *fugu* might well be a way of turning the tide of Western attitudes to offal in general. While it is currently only in vogue among gourmets and chefs, it is possible that their enthusiasm will gradually filter through to the majority, as is the way with many a fashion.

7
Leftovers

There are many non-culinary uses for offal: as tallow for candles, rendered for soap, in chemical and pharmaceutical applications, in ancient and New Age medicine and so on. The Inuit use seal guts for making underwear and Arctic peoples use the intestines of bears, walruses and sea lions to construct raincoats.[1] They may be practical but can be strangely beautiful, intricately pleated and luminous. Grasses are sewn into the seams so that when the coat is wet the grass swells and the vulnerable seams remain watertight. Some of these coats are designed to be wide at the base so they can be tied across the opening of a kayak to keep the wearer dry during rain or rough seas. The sculptor Mary-Anne Wensley draws on this tradition by using dried pig intestines to construct her ethereal structures.[2]

Today many beauty potions are derived from offal, such as collagen to plump up ageing skin, which leads us to the bbc tv series *Absolutely Fabulous* (1992), in which the teenaged Saffy is scornful when ageing model Patsy tries out a new beauty cure-all: 'You look like a haggis with pointed toes. A tight old bladder skin holding together some rotting offal.'

The *Ministry of Food* exhibition at the Imperial War Museum in London in 2010 displayed a mesh-lined bucket

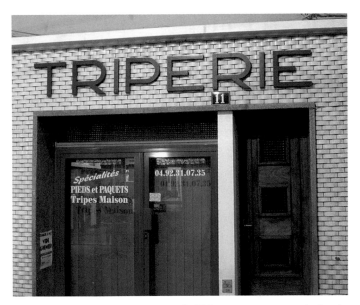

A specialist tripe shop in Nice, many of which are now permanently closed.

used for preserving eggs in a solution of isinglass. During the Second World War such preserved eggs would have been a welcome alternative to the powdered kind. Dissolved in water, the resulting solution coated the eggs, stopping air from permeating their shells. Unfortunately the process affected the taste of the eggs and the shells could no longer stand up to boiling. Isinglass is made from the swim bladders of fish, and is a form of collagen that was previously used to clarify wine and beer. It is also a specialized form of glue, used in manuscript conservation to repair parchment when mixed with honey or glycerin. It can be a gelling agent in jelly, desserts, confectionery and blancmange. Originally made from Russian sturgeon and thus prohibitively expensive, in 1795 isinglass was successfully obtained from cod and began to be used more widely.

Goat's bladder was used for condoms in ancient Rome and pig's and sheep's intestines may have been used as such in ancient Egypt. There is evidence that early Chinese condoms, covering only the head of the penis, were made from lamb's intestines.

Offal can also be rendered for use as a fertilizer, which can in turn enrich the soil to grow animal feed to support livestock, which comes full circle to provide yet more offal.

In an age when we are encouraged not to be wasteful, with the weight of ecological breakdown bearing down upon us, it seems a pity that offal is so often disregarded by meat eaters, for reasons that can be hard to articulate. The Slow Food Movement, with its Terra Madre network of food communities, founded by Carlo Petrini in 1986, supports the idea of using locally sourced produce for food to retain its character, and safeguarding the quality of life of the animal. Since offal tastes better when fresh, this is good news for offal eaters.

Offal is traditional and fashionable, Eastern and Western, humble and refined, of religious and medical significance. It is medicine and love potion and sometimes a troubling idea. It is affordable, healthy food, delicious in all its variety.

Recipes

Noumbles
—from Samuel Pegge, *The Forme of Cury* (1390)

Take noumbles of deer other of other beest parboile hem kerf
hem to dyce. tak brede and grynde with the broth. and temper it
up with a gode quantite of vyneger and wyne. take the onyouns
and parboyle hem. and mynce hem smale and do þer to. colour it
with blode and do þer to powdour fort and salt and boyle it wele
and serue it forth.

Calf's tripe, or Charpie
—from *The Viandier of Taillevent* (c. 1395)

Take your meat when it is completely cooked, cut it up very small,
and fry it in lard. Crush ginger and saffron. Beat some raw eggs
and thread them onto your meat in the lard. Crush spices and add
some spice powder. However, some do not wish any spice powder in it, and eat it with green verjuice.

Blewe manger (brawn)

—from *A Proper newe Booke of Cokerye*, mid-16th century (Cambridge, 1913), ed. Catherine Frances Frere

Take a capon and cut out the brawne of hym a lyve and perboyle the brawne till the flesshe come from the bone, and then drye hym as you canne, in a fayre clothe, then take a payre of cardes and carde hym as small as is possyble, and than take a pottell of mylke and a pottell of creame, and halfe a pounde of Rye flower, and your carded brawne of the capon and put all into a pan, and stere it al together and set it upon the fyre, and whan it begynneth to boyle put thereto halfe a pounde of beaten Suger and a sauser-full of Rose water and so let it boyle tyll it be very thicke, then put it into a charger tyll it be colde, and then ye may slyce it as ye doe lieche and so serve it in.

Blood Pudding

—from *The Acomplish'd Lady's Delight in Preserving, Physick, Beautifying and Cookery* (1675)

Take a quart of Sheep'd blood, and a quart of Cream, ten Eggs, the yolks and the whites beaten together; stir all this Liquor very well, then thicken it with grated bread, and Oat-meal finely beaten, of each a like quantity, Beef-suet finely shred, and Marrow in little lumps, season it with a little Nutmeg, Cloves, and Mace mingled with salt, a little sweet Marjoram, Thyme, and Penny-royal shred very well together, and mingle them with the other things, some put in a few Currans: Then fill them in cleansed Guts, and boyl them very carefully.

Marrow Pudding

—from John Nott, *The Cooks and Confectioners Dictionary* (1723)

Cut 2 French rolls into Slices, and take a quarter of a Pound of coarse Bisket, put into a Saucepan a Quart of Milk, set it over the

Fire, make it Blood warm, and pour it upon your Bread; cover it close and let it soak, 'till it is cold; rub it through a Cullender, mince half a Pound of Marrow, and put to it three Eggs well beaten and strained; then mix all together; sweeten with the sugar; add a little Salt, and a Spoonful or two of Rose-water, scrape in a little Nutmeg, put in two Ounces of Almonds well pownded; mix all these well together, put them into Guts, and tie them up; but do not fill them too full; Boil them in Water for a quarter of an Hour, turning them with a Skimmer; lay them in a Cullender to cool: When you use them, put them into a Pan with a little Butter, and fry them as yellow as Gold, or you may set them in the Mouth of an Oven. These are proper to garnish a boil'd Pudding, or a fricassy of Chickens, for the first Course, or you may serve them in little Dishes or Plates for the second Course.

Battalia Pie
—from Susannah Carter, *The Frugal Housewife* (1772). 'Battalia' or 'batalia' is from the French *béatilles*, from Latin *beatillae*, meaning small, blessed objects.

Take 4 small chickens and squab pigeons, four sucking rabbits, cut them into pieces and season them with savoury spice, lay them in a pie with 4 sweetbreads sliced, as many sheep's tongues and shivered palates, 2 pair of lamb's stones, 20 or 30 cockscombs, with savoury balls and oysters; lay on butter and lose the pie with a lear [gravy].

A Fricasey of Lamb-Stones and Sweetbreads
—from Hannah Glasse, *The Art of Cookery Made Plain and Easy* (1774)

Have some lamb-stones blanched, parboiled and sliced, and flour 2 or 3 sweetbreads; if very thick cut them into 2, the yolks of 6 hard eggs whole; a few pistachio nut kernels, and a few large oysters: fry them all of a fine brown, then pour out all the butter, and add a pint of drawn gravy, the lamb-stones, some asparagus tops about an inch long, some grated nutmeg, a little pepper and salt, 2 shallots shred small, and a glass of white wine. Stew all together for 10 minutes, then add the yolks of 6 eggs beat very fine, with a little white wine, and a little beaten mace; stir altogether till it is of a fine thickness, then dish it up. Garnish with lemon.

Lamb's Head and Pluck
—from William Kitchener, *Apicius Redivivus* (1817)

Clean and wash a lamb's head well, and boil it an hour and a half: take it up, and rub it over with a paste brush dipped in egg well beaten; strew over it a little pepper and salt, and some fine bread crumbs: lay it in a dish before the fire, or in a Dutch oven to brown: when it begins to get dry, put some melted butter on it with a paste brush: mince the heart, liver and the tongue very fine; put them into a stewpan with a little of the liquor the head was boiled in, and an ounce of butter, well mixed with a tablespoonful of flour, a little pepper and salt: set it on a slow fire for ten minutes. Squeeze the juice of half a lemon into a dish, lay in the mince, with the head upon it, and garnish it with relishing rashers of bacon.

Pig's Pettitoes (trotters)
—from *Mrs Beeton's Book of Household Management* (London, 1861)

Ingredients: A thin slice of bacon, 1 onion, 1 blade of mace, 6 peppercorns, 3 or 4 sprigs of thyme, 1 pint of gravy, pepper and salt to taste, thickening of butter and flour.

Mode: Put the liver, heart and pettitoes into a stewpan with the bacon, mace, peppercorns, thyme, onion and gravy, and simmer these gently for ¼ hour; then take out the heart and liver and mince them very fine. Keep stewing the feet until quite tender, which will be in 20 minutes to ½ hour, reckoning from the time that they boiled up first; then put back the minced liver, thicken the gravy with a little butter and flour, season with pepper and salt, and over a gentle fire for 5 minutes, occasionally stirring the contents. Dish the mince, split the feet, and pour the gravy in the middle.

Turkey Giblets with Turnips
—from the Marquis de Courchamps, in Alexandre Dumas' *Dictionary of Cuisine* (Paris, 1871)

Clean the wings, gizzards, feet and neck, discarding the head; place in a large pan on the heat with a good piece of butter kneaded with flour; sauté the offal for 7 to 8 minutes; add hot stock, being careful not to blend it into your roux too quickly; add in a bouquet of parsley, thyme, bay leaf, basil and sage, together with 2 onions stuck with cloves, boil for a quarter of an hour and then add 6 Fresneuse turnips, 4 large slices of carrot, 6 purple potatoes, a Jerusalem artichoke and a whole stalk of celery; do not turn your vegetables, just keep them moving a little or the dish would soon lose its air of bourgeois simplicity and natural grace; skim away any fat carefully after about 1½ hours of slow simmer, arrange your vegetables around the giblets, with the wings in place of honour; then so that the potatoes keep your sauce unctuous, pass it through a sieve.

Pig's Harslet
—from *Mrs A. B. Marshall's Cookery Book* (1888)

Wash and dry some liver, sweetbreads and fat and bits of pork, beating the latter with a rolling pin to make it tender; season with pepper, salt, sage and a little onion shred fine; when mixed, put all into a caul, and fasten it up tight with a needle and thread. Roast it on a hanging-jack or by a string.

Or serve in slices with parsley for a fry. Serve with a sauce of port-winer and water, and mustard, just boiled up and put into a dish.

Ox-tail en Hochepot
—from Prosper Montagné, *Larousse Gastronomique* (1900)

Cut the ox-tail, whether skinned or not, into uniform chunks. Put into a stock-pot with 2 raw pig's trotters, each cut into 4 or 5 pieces, and a whole raw pig's ear. Add enough water to cover, bring to the boil, remove scum and simmer gently for 2 hours. Add a small cabbage cut into quarters and blanched, 3 carrots, 2 turnips, in quarters or cut into small uniform pieces, and 10 small onions. Simmer gently for 2 hours. Drain the pieces of ox-tail and the pig's trotters. Arrange them on a large, deep, round dish. Put the vegetables in the middle. Surround with grilled chipolata sausages and the pig's ear cut into strips. Serve boiled potatoes separately.

Blanquette of Calves' Hearts
—from Sarah Tyson Rorer, *Mrs Rorer's New Cook Book*
(Philadelphia, *c.* 1902)

Wash two calves' hearts thoroughly in cold water; cut them into cubes of one inch. Put them into a saucepan; cover with boiling water, bring to a boil, skim and simmer gently for two hours. When ready to serve rub together two tablespoonfuls of butter and two of flour; add the liquor in which the hearts were cooked; stir until boiling; add a teaspoonful of salt and a saltspoonful of pepper. Take from the fire, add the yolks of two eggs. Dish the hearts and pour over the sauce. Garnish the dish with carefully boiled rice, and send it at once to the table. This makes an exceedingly nice dish for lunch. A heavy rope or garnish of nicely cooked green peas outside of the rice makes it more sightly.

Foie Gras

—from Auguste Escoffier's *The Complete Guide to the Art of Modern Cookery*, trans. H. L. Cracknell and R. J. Kaufmann (New York, 1997)

For serving as a hot dish the goose liver should firstly be well trimmed and the nerves removed; it is then studded with quarters of small raw peeled truffles which have been seasoned with salt and pepper, quickly set and stiffened over heat with a little brandy together with a bay-leaf. Before using the truffles leave them to cool in a tightly closed terrine. After the foie gras has been studded wrap it completely in slices of pork fat or pig's caul, and place in a tightly closed terrine for a few hours.

Brain Fritters

—from Misses A. and M. Schauer, *The Schauer Cookery Book* (Brisbane and Sydney, 1909)

Carefully wash an ox brain, and boil it for a quarter of an hour in well-seasoned stock. When the brain is cold, cut it into slices, dip each of them in batter, drop them as you do them into a pan half full of smoking fat. To make the batter, mix two large table-spoonfuls of fine flour with four of cold water, stir in a table-spoonful of dissolved butter, the yolk of an egg and a pinch of salt and pepper; when ready to use beat the white of an egg to a strong froth, and mix with it. As you take them up, throw them on paper to absorb any grease clinging to them, serve on a napkin or ornamental dish-paper.

Roasted Foie Gras with Crispy Chicken Skin, Chicken Heart Gravy, Peppercorn Biscuit and Spiced Honey
—Jesse Schenker, 2012

1 lb (450 g) grade A foie gras (portioned into around 15 pieces)
1 cup (250 g) chicken hearts
1 cup (250 g) cleaned, soaked chicken livers
Skin of 2 large chickens (attached as much as possible)
2 cups (470 ml) whole milk
¼ cup (60 g) all purpose flour
¼ cup (60 g) whole butter
1 tablespoon chopped thyme
1 clove chopped garlic
1 large shallot diced
1 cup (235 ml) clover honey
2 tablespoons Activa (meat glue)
7 sheets of silver gelatine
1 tablespoon extra virgin olive oil
Pinch of cayenne pepper
Kosher salt to taste
2 quarts (2 l) of grape seed oil for frying
For biscuits:
1.5 cups (375 g) plain (all-purpose) flour
1 teaspoon salt
1 teaspoon sugar
1 teaspoon baking powder
1 teaspoon crushed pink peppercorns
2.5 tablespoons butter cut into half-inch cubes
½ cup (118 ml) cream

For chicken skin
(Recommended 24 hours prior)
Spread chicken skin on perforated rack with drip pan and salt heavily. Place in refrigerator overnight.

For spiced honey

In saucepot, add honey, half of the shallots, garlic and thyme. Put on super low heat and let steep for 1 hour. Strain into a bowl and put aside.

For chicken-heart filling

In a large saucepot, put butter and flour on medium heat and whisk for 3–5 minutes until golden roux forms. In a separate saucepot, heat milk just below a simmer. Once roux is ready, add hot milk whisking slowly into roux to form béchamel. Lower heat and stir every couple of minutes to let the sauce thicken. In a large cast-iron pan, heat olive oil to high heat and brown chicken hearts and chicken livers. Add the remainder of the garlic, thyme and shallot and cook until everything is soft and the organs are golden brown. Place in a bowl and set aside.

Once organ mixture is cooled, rough chop contents on a cutting board into small pieces. Be careful not to over chop or leave too large. Place contents into béchamel on stove and stir thoroughly. The mixture should be a little bit thinner than wallpaper paste. Incorporate bloomed gelatine to mixture. Mix thoroughly. Season with salt and cayenne pepper. Pour into a thin pan and place in the refrigerator for 3 hours or until set.

For biscuits

Mix all of ingredients together in a bowl. Add the cubed butter and use a bench scraper or 2 knives to cut the butter into lentil-sized pieces throughout the dry ingredients. Pour in the cream and mix until it just comes together.

Chill the dough for 1 hour in fridge and roll out into a 1-inch-thick disc. Use a ½-inch circle cutter to make small cylinders. Bake at 350°F (180°C) for 8 minutes or until golden-brown on the bottom.

To finish chicken skin

Rinse salt off chicken skin and dry in between paper towels very well. Cut with scissors into 2 inch × 2 inch (5 x 5 cm) squares. Take one piece of plastic wrap and lay chicken skin on top. Dust with a thin layer of meat glue (we recommend using an icing (powered) sugar dispenser) ensuring you cover all four corners of the chicken skin. With a small melon-baller or teaspoon, set a dollop of chicken gravy in the centre. Fold all four corners of the chicken skin into the centre and then lift the plastic up and twist tightly to form a snug ball. Tie with an additional piece of plastic so the ball stays extremely tight. Place in fridge for 1 hour. After 1 hour, place chicken balls in boiling water for 5 minutes and then shock in an ice bath to stop the cooking (make sure you cook the chicken skin fully in boiling water).

To finish
Remove plastic from chicken ball and place in 350°F (180°C) fryer. Fry for 2–3 minutes or until golden-brown. Salt foie gras and roast in cast-iron pan until golden-brown. Lightly warm the biscuit in the oven.

To plate
With a spoon, drizzle some of the spiced honey on a plate. Place the foie gras, the biscuit and chicken ball on the plate and serve immediately. Optional garnish: bitter lettuce.

Pig's Ear and Pork Chop Pie
—Sham Kesar-Bramall of Little Chilli Catering, 2012

Pastry
100 g plain flour
45 g butter
salt

Add the above to a food processor and blitz up until you have breadcrumbs. Add cold water slowly until the pastry comes together. Chill for 30 minutes until use.

Pie filling
1 pig's ear, cut into large strips roughly 10 cm long and 3 cm wide
300 g pork chop, sliced into 2 cm strips
2 onions, diced
1 stalk celery, finely diced
2 cloves garlic, finely chopped
250 ml white wine
300 ml chicken stock
1 lemon, zest only
sage to season
1 small red chilli, diced finely
50 g butter
1 egg to brush pastry

Fry off the onions, garlic and celery for 5 minutes. Add stock and white wine and simmer for 15–20 minutes. Add the pig's ear strips and simmer for 1–2 hours, topping up with hot water if necessary. Remove the pig's ear from the stock and cut into strips as thinly as possible. Fry in the butter and season with salt and pepper (fry half of the strips until crisp and fry the other half until slightly less crisp as these will top the pie later and get cooked again in the oven). Fry off the pork chop pieces in butter, season with sage, salt and pepper and add to the stock. Fill a medium-sized pie dish with the pork chop and stock and sprinkle half of the pig's ears on top. Line the top with the pastry and press onto the sides of the dish to seal. Prick a hole in the middle of the pie and brush with egg. Sprinkle the rest of the pig's ear strips on top of the pastry. Cook at 200°C for 15–20 minutes or until the pie has browned.

Devilled Kidneys

4 pieces of toast
8 sheep's kidneys
2 oz (60 g) butter
1 tablespoon mustard powder
1 dessertspoon Worcester Sauce
salt and pepper

Carefully remove the skin from the kidneys, rinse in cold water and pat dry, cut in half and core. Mix together the mustard and sauce. Heat the butter in a pan and add the kidneys, season with salt and pepper and brown for about 2 minutes. Lower the heat and cook gently for 5 minutes with the pan covered. Add the mustard/sauce mixture and braise gently for a little longer. Serve on hot toast.

Thai Spicy Pig Organ Soup
—Atitaya Chewasuwan, 2011

Bring to the boil with a pint of water a handful of mixed pig offal with lime leaves, galangal, fish sauce and a pinch of sugar. Then add lemon grass, chopped spring onion, chilli and coriander. Simple, fragrant and delicious.

References

Introduction

1 Joan Alcock, *Food in the Ancient World* (Westport, CT, 2006), p. 65.
2 Maguelonne Toussaint-Samat, *A History of Food* (Oxford, 1987), p. 424.
3 Plutarch, *Life of Lycurgus*, 2:2.
4 In Aristophanes' *The Birds*, for example, Prometheus cries 'If Zeus sees me down here I'm a dead liver'; the Thracians threaten to march against Zeus unless he opens up the ports so that they can import their 'beloved offal pieces' again. (Act 2, trans. G. Theodoridis, 2005).
5 Athanaeus in *Deipnosophistae*, cited in Toussaint-Samat, *History of Food*, p. 425.
6 In Cato's *De Agri Cultura*, 89.
7 Pliny the Elder, *De Natura Rerum*, Book 10. 26.
8 Alan Davidson, *The Oxford Companion to Food* (Oxford, 1999), p. 84.
9 Cited in Andrew Dalby, *Food in the Ancient World from A–Z* (London, 2003), p. 208: Homer, *Iliad* 22.501, *Odyssey* 9.293.
10 Dimitra Karamanides, *Pythagoras* (New York, 2006), p. 5.
11 Lawrence D. Kritzman, in *Food: A Culinary History* (New York, 1996), quotes Seneca's criticism, singling out a vogue for flamingos' tongues.
12 Isidore of Seville, *Etymologies* 20:5–7.

13 Athanaeus (*Deipnosophistae*, Book 3) mentions the gourmand Callimedon, so called because he leapt like a crayfish for a dish of tripe. Dioxippus mocks his catholic taste: 'What dishes he hankers after! How refined they are! Sweetbreads, paunches, entrails!'

14 Mireille Corbier, 'The Broad Bean and the Moray: Social Hierachies and Food in Rome', in *Food: A Culinary History*, ed. Jean-Louis Flandrin and Massimo Montanari, trans. Albert Sonnenfeld (New York, 1999). Andrew Dalby refers to Plutarch regarding the higher order delicacy of miscarried sow's womb, achieved by jumping on the pregnant animal, to savour the meat at its most tender phase – a technique also benefiting the udder, *Food in the Ancient World*, p. 360.

1 Definitions and Ideas

1 *The New Oxford American Dictionary* at least lists the edible definition first:

> 'the entrails and internal organs of an animal used as food.

.   • refuse or waste material.

> • decomposing animal flesh.
>
> ORIGIN late Middle English (in the sense [refuse from a process]): probably suggested by Middle Dutch *afval*, from *af "off"* + *vallen "to fall."*'

2 Bath chaps, or chaps, are the lower portions of a pig's cheek, and include the jaw meat, boned, formed into a cone which is cut vertically, salted and smoked and sometimes rolled in breadcrumbs. 'Chap' is a variant of chop; 'Bath' is probably part of the name because the cut originates from that part of southern England, and was originally made from the Gloucestershire Old Spot pig. Haslet was defined by Dr Johnson in 1755 as 'heart, liver and lights of a hog, with the windpipe and part of the throat to it'. Alan Davidson in the *Oxford Companion to Food* (Oxford, 1999) describes haslet today as being a dish of finely chopped offal, cooked as a

meatloaf covered with kidney fat (flead) or caul. Chine is the meat surrounding the backbone of an animal, the word coming from fourteeth-century French, *eschine*.

3　In contrast Sophocles uses 'white marrow' as a poetic euphemism for brains. In *The Trachinian Women* Heracles throw Lichas into the sea, spilling his brains upon the water: 'He spilled the white marrow from the hair, when the head was split in the middle and blood spurted forth with it.'

4　In *Shark's Fin and Sichuan Pepper: A Sweet-Sour Memoir of Eating in China* (London, 2008), Fuschia Dunlop admits 'in my stomach of stomachs I remained an observer', p. 135.

5　Douglas Houston's poem 'With the Offal Eaters' in the collection of the same name (London, 1986).

6　Tara Austen Weaver wrote recently of her sudden switch to meat-eating to treat hyperthyroidism after a vegetarian childhood. Email to author (2 February 2010).

7　Jonathan Miller, *The Body in Question* (London, 1980), p. 24.

8　Mary Douglas, *Annual Report of the Russell Sage Foundation* (1978), p. 59.

9　Elizabeth David, *A Book of Mediterranean Food* (1950).

10　Miller, *The Body in Question*, p. 24.

11　Fergus Henderson, *Nose to Tail Eating* (London, 1999), p. 62.

2　The Offal Tradition

1　USDA tracks offal exports to China, including Hong Kong, in 2001 as being $59 million worth in red meat offal; $135 million in poultry paws (which are the feet minus the spurs); and $41 million in poultry offal, these figures mounting steadily to 2011. Since 2008, China has even rivalled exports to Mexico, and in 2010 32 per cent of all US pork variety meats were exported to China. Most liver exports still go to Russia. (Global Trade Information Service, 2011).

2　Marco Polo, and Henry Yule, trans. and ed., *The Book of Ser Marco Polo, the Venetian: Concerning the Kingdoms and the Marvels of the East*, Book 2, p. 40.

3 Gillian Kendall, *Mr Ding's Chicken Feet* (Madison, WI, 2006),
   p. 116.

4 Fuchsia Dunlop, *Shark's Fin and Sichuan Pepper: A Sweet-Sour
   Memoir of Eating in China* (London, 2008), p. 58.

5 Shizuo Tsuji and M.F.K. Fisher, *Japanese Cooking: A Simple
   Art* (1998), p. 259.

6 Penny Van Esterik, *Food Culture in Southeast Asia*
   (London, 2008), p. 25.

7 The food writer Tom Parker-Bowles, travelling in Laos on
   the hunt for foods he found challenging, found that the
   smell of what he was eating was a significant factor.

8 Khammaan Khonkhai, trans. Gehan Wijeyewardene,
   The Teachers of Mad Dog Swamp [1978] (Chiang Mai, 1992).

9 Maxime Rodinson et al., *Medieval Arab Cookery*, trans.
   Charles Perry (Totnes, 2001), p. 373.

10 Anissa Helou, *The Fifth Quarter: An Offal Cookbook*
   (London, 2004), p. 8; Anissa Helou, email to author
   (14 April 2011).

11 Nevin Halıcı (1989) cited in Alan Davidson, *The Oxford
   Companion to Food* (Oxford, 1999), p. 808.

12 Tess Mallos, *The Complete Middle East Cookbook* (London,
   1995), p. 105.

13 Abdel-Moneim Said, 'Wasting Ramadan' in *Al-Ahram*, 963
   (3–9 September 2009), cites government figures showing
   the tendency in Egypt for even the poor to overspend on
   food during Ramadan, by as much as 50–100 per cent of
   their usual food outlay.

14 Arto der Haroutunian, *North African Cookery* (London, 2009),
   p. 183.

15 Sofia Larrinúa-Craxton, *The Mexican Mama's Kitchen*
   (London, 2005).

16 Elisabeth Luard, *The Latin American Kitchen* (London, 2002).

3 The West

1 Richard J. Hooker, *Food and Drink in America* (Indianapolis, IN, 1981), p. 56.

2 Hiram Chittenden, *The American Fur Trade of the Far West* (Lincoln, NE, 1986), vol. II, p. 805.

3 Hooker, *Food and Drink in America*, p. 183.

4 The first American Testicle Festival took place in Montana in 1982. Originally 300 took part, but when 15,000 attended in 2010 it became something of a tourist-fest — akin to haggis festivals in Scotland and French *andouillette fêtes*.

5 Clare Ansberry, 'Cue the Music! Liver Lovers Shiver at the Dish's Decline,' *Wall Street Journal*, 14 April 2011.

6 Sally Fallon, 'Australian Aborigines: Living Off the Fat of the Land', *Nourished Magazine* (December 2008), suggests an alternative possibility: that offal might have been eaten first simply because it went off first.

7 The dentist-nutritionist Weston Price's ethnographic travels in the 1930s support the idea that Aborigines recognized their need for fat-rich variety meat.

8 Sarah Josepha Hale, *The Ladies' New Book of Cookery* (1852), p. 14.

9 *The Pall Mall Gazette*, cited in Kenneth James, *Escoffier: The King of Chefs* (London, 2006), p. 57.

10 Waverley Root, *The Food of France* (London, 1983).

11 Alan Davidson, *The Oxford Companion to Food* (Oxford, 1999), p. 261.

12 John Cooper, *Eat and Be Satisfied: A Social History of Jewish Food* (Lanham, MD, 1993), p. 422.

13 Gil Marks, *The Encyclopedia of Jewish Food* (Princeton, NJ, 2010), p. 601.

14 Cooper, *Eat and Be Satisfied*, p. 192.

15 Michèle Brown, *Eating Like a King* (London, 2006) .

16 William Cobbett, *Rural Rides* (London, 1830), entry for Burghclere, Hampshire, Monday, 2 October 1826.

17 William Cobbett, 'Not by Bullets and Bayonets', *Cobbett's Writings on the Irish Question* (London, 1795–1835).

18 Sarah Winman, 'A Lesson in Tripe', *Spitalfields Life*,
   1 March 2011.
19 Mrs Beeton, *Everyday Cookery* (London, 1861), p. 178.
20 Marguerite Patten, *Post War Kitchen* (London, 1998).
21 Marco Polo, and Henry Yule, trans. and ed., *The Book of Ser
   Marco Polo, the Venetian: Concerning the Kingdoms and the Marvels
   of the East* (Cambridge, 1999), p. 231.
22 Originally a medieval feast, the celebration of Þorrablót had
   waned, and was revived in the late 1950s by a Reykjavík
   restaurant specializing in traditional food.
23 See http://vimeo.com5590685 for a scene in the film adap-
   tation of Arnaldur Indriðason's *Jar City* (Baltasar Kormákur,
   2006), in which Inspector Erlander sits quietly at his
   kitchen table eating half a pickled sheep's head.
24 *Gestgjafinn*, 'Feast Days and Food Days', at
   www.gestgjafinn.is/english/nr/352.
25 Sharon Hudgins, *The Other Side of Russia: A Slice of Life in
   Siberia and the Russian Far East* (College Station, TX, 2003),
   p. 138.
26 Thomas Keller, *The French Laundry Cookbook* (London,
   1999).

4 Macho Status

1 Charlotte Du Cann in *Offal and the New Brutalism* (London,
  1985) examines the boisterous British macho culture of the
  1980s.
2 Barbara Pym, *Jane and Prudence* (London, 1953), p. 21. The
  idea that men require meat is a recurring conceit in Pym's
  novels.
3 Julie Powell, *Cleaving* (New York, 2009), p. 64, in a recipe
  for blood sausage.
4 Stephanie Diani, *Offal Taste* photo series at
  www.eatmedaily.
  com, April 2009.
5 Dale Kramer, in 'Hardy and Readers: *Jude the Obscure*', in

The Cambridge Companion to Thomas Hardy (Cambridge, 1999), ed. Kramer, describes the censorship that Hardy faced when publishing the novel in serial form in *Harper's Magazine* in 1895, where he had 'drastically diminished the pig-killing scene, evidently because American readers had recently been offended by reports of cruelty to animals on Western ranches', pp. 166–7. This might be seen as evidence of late nineteenth-century sensibility towards the brute facts of slaughter and towards offal in particular.

6 Diane Cardwell, 'A Dining Club for Those With Adventurous Stomachs', *New York Times*, 8 July 2010.
7 Giles Coren, 'Cay Tre: Chicken Gizzard and Muop is a Hell of a Name, but English People Don't Like Eating Gizzards', *The Times*, 29 September 2007.
8 Clarissa Dickson Wright, *The Haggis: A Short History* (Belfast, 1998).
9 'The Horace Poem', in *Monty Python's Big Red Book* (London, 1980).
10 James Meikle, 'Hands Off Our Haggis, Say Scots After English Claim', *Guardian*, 3 August 2009.
11 Alexander McCall Smith, 'Keep Your Hands Off Our Haggis', *New York Times,* 6 August 2009.

5 As Ritual

1 Andrew Dalby, *Food in the Ancient World from A–Z* (London, 2003), p. 288. Dalby relates how having to cook and eat the meat directly after slaughter and sacrifice was not ideal from the gourmet perspective, and that Plutarch suggests hanging the meat in a fig tree before cooking to solve the culinary problem.
2 The Truth and Reconciliation Commission, 2008.
3 Ed Vulliamy, 'Srebrenića: Genocide and Memory', *Open Democracy*, 9 June 2012.
4 Claude Lévi-Strauss, *The Raw and the Cooked* (London, 1986), pp. 241–4.

5 James Bradley, *Flyboys* (New York, 2007), pp. 519–20.

6 According to Alan Davidson, *The Oxford Companion to Food* (Oxford, 1999), p. 83, blood-tapping is a traditional custom for nomadic tribes such as Berbers and Monguls because it was an available renewable resource. The Masai obtain blood by firing an arrow at close range into a vein in the neck of their cattle, and the wound is then plugged; Martin Jones in *A History of the World in 100 Objects*, presented by Neil MacGregor of the British Museum, on BBC Radio 4, January 2010.

7 Malcolm Margolin, 'The Ohlone Way: Indian Life in the San Francisco Bay Area,' cited in Sage Dilts, 'Eating Offal', *Edible East Bay* (Spring 2011).

8 Inga Clendinnen in *Aztecs: An Interpretation* (Cambridge, 1991) cites the Christian missionary W. H. Prescott, who wrote in the early 1840s of his distaste, not for the killings themselves, but for the inappropriate nature of the subsequent feast, for its not being 'the coarse repast of famished cannibals . . . Surely, never was refinement and the extreme of barbarism brought so closely into contact with each other.' Clendinnen throws doubt on his interpretation.

9 *Unani* or *unani-tibbi* literally translates as 'Greek medicine'. It is built on the teaching of Hippocrates and Galen and was further developed in the Islamic world.

10 Ambrose Bierce, *The Devil's Dictionary* (London, 1911).

11 John Platt, 'South African Gamblers Smoke Endangered Vulture Brains for Luck', *Scientific American*, 10 June 2010.

12 Norman Lewis, *Naples '44* (London, 1978).

6 As Medicine

1 Mark Grant, *Galen on Food and Diet* (London, 2000), p. 160–62.

2 Vivienne Lo, 'Pleasure, Prohibition and Pain: Food and Medicine in Traditional China', in *Tripod and Palate*, ed. Roel Sterckx (New York, 2005), p. 174, cites Hu Sihui's *Propriety*

and Essentials in Eating and Drinking, completed in 1330.

3 John Cooper, *Eat and Be Satisfied: A Social History of Jewish Food* (Lanham, MD, 1993). By 'eating different portions of an animal, the corresponding part of the human body would be strengthened, but an exception was made for the heart, brain and liver', p. 127.

4 Li Shizhen's *Bencao Gangmu* was finished in 1578 and provides the most extensive pharmaceutical record of Chinese medicine, including recipes and illustrations, and advice about where to find the best quality animals for different purposes and the uses and medical effects of their offal parts..

5 'Why Eat a Placenta?', *BBC News Magazine*, 18 April 2006.

6 International Commission on Microbiological Specifications for Foods, ed., *Microbial Ecology of Food Commodities* (New York, 2005).

7 Roger Kelsey, Chief Executive of the NFMFT, email to the author, 3 March 2011.

8 Anil Aggrawal, 'Death By Vitamin A', in *The Poison Sleuths*, October 1999.

9 Norimitsu Onishi, 'If the Fish Liver Can't Kill, Is it Really a Delicacy?', *New York Times*, 4 May 2008.

10 Tamao Noguchi, marine toxin specialist from Tokyo Healthcare University, cited ibid.

7 Leftovers

1 J.C.H. King, Birgit Pautsztat and Robert Storrie, *Arctic Clothing* (Montreal, 2005).

2 Mary-Anne Wensley's *Inescapable Shelter* of 2009 is a shed-sized structure rather like a translucent beehive, for which she needed 2,700 pig intestine bricks.

Select Bibliography

Albala, Ken, *Food in Early Modern Europe* (Westport, CT, 2003)

Alcock, Joan P., *Food in the Ancient World* (Santa Barbara, CA, 2006)

Allen, Jana and Gin, Margaret, *Offal* (London, 1976)

Apicius, Cookery and Dining in Imperial Rome, trans. Joseph Dommers Vehling [1936] (New York 1977)

Artusi, Pellegrino, *The Science of Cookery and the Art of Eating Well* (Florence, 1891)

Austen Weaver, Tara, *The Butcher and the Vegetarian* (New York, 2010)

Barlow, John, *Everything but the Squeal* (London, 2008)

Beeton, Mrs, *Mrs Beeton's Everyday Cookery* [1861] (London, 1963)

Blechman, Andrew D., 'For German Butchers: A Wurst Case Scenario', *The Smithsonian* (January 2010)

Brothwell, Don R. and Patricia Brothwell, *Food in Antiquity* (Baltimore, MD, 1998)

Brown, Michèle, *Eating Like a King* (London, 2006)

Cannizzaro, Liza, *The Art of Having Guts* (San Francisco, CA, 2007)

Carême, Marie-Antoine, *L'Art de la Cuisine au XIXe Siècle* (Paris, 1833–7)

Carluccio, Antonio, *Italia: The Recipes and Customs of the Regions* (London, 2007)

Chittenden, Hiram Martin, *The American Fur Trade of the Far West* [1935] (Nebraska, NE, 1986)

Cooper, John, *Eat and Be Satisfied: A Social History of Jewish Food* (Lanham, MD, 1993)

Corbier, Mireille, 'The Broad Bean and the Moray: Social
    Hierachies and Food in Rome', in *Food: A Culinary History*,
    ed. Jean-Louis Flandrin and Massimo Montanari, trans.
    Albert Sonnenfeld (New York, 1999)
Dalby, Andrew, *Food in the Ancient World from A–Z* (London, 2003)
Davidson, Alan, *The Oxford Companion to Food* (Oxford, 1999)
Douglas, Mary, *Purity and Danger* (London, 1966)
Douglas, Norman (Pilaff Bey), *Venus in the Kitchen* (Kingswood,
    Surrey, 1952)
Dowell, Philip and Bailey, Adrian, *The Book of Ingredients*
    (London, 1980)
Dumas, Alexandre, *Grand Dictionnaire de Cuisine* (Paris, 1873)
Du Cann, Charlotte, *Offal and the New Brutalism* (London, 1985)
Dunlop, Fuchsia, *Shark's Fin and Sichuan Pepper* (London, 2008)
Emin-Tunc, Tanfer, 'Black and White Breakfast', *Bright Lights
    Film Journal*, 38 (2002)
Fearnley-Whittingstall, Hugh, *The River Cottage Meat Book*
    (London, 2004)
Fernández-Armesto, Felipe, *Food: A History* (London, 2001)
Fiddes, Nick, 'Social Aspects of Meat Eating', *Proceedings of the
    Nutrition Society*, 53 (1994), pp. 271–80
Fitzgibbon, Theodora, *The Food of the Western World* (London,
    1976)
Freedman, Paul H., *Food: The History of Taste* (Berkeley, CA, 2007)
—, *Out of the East: Spices and the Medieval Imagination* (New Haven,
    CT, 2009)
Grant, Mark, *Galen on Food and Diet* (London, 2000)
Halicí, Nevin, *Nevin Halici's Turkish Cookbook* (London, 1993)
Haroutunian, Arto der, *North African Cookery* (London, 1985)
Heath, Ambrose, *Meat* (London, 1971)
Helou, Anissa, *The Fifth Quarter: An Offal Cookbook* (London,
    2004)
Henderson, Fergus, with an introduction by Anthony Bourdain,
    The Whole Beast: Nose to Tail Eating (London, 2004)
Hieatt, Constance B., and Sharon Butler, *Pleyn Delit* (Toronto,
    1976)
Hooda, Fateema, *Khoja Khana* (New Delhi, 2002)

Hooker, Richard J., *Food and Drink in America* (Indianapolis, IN, 1981)

Karamanides, Dimitra, *Pythagoras* (New York, 2006)

Keijzer Brackman, Agnes de, and Cathy Brackman, *Cook Indonesian* (Singapore, 2005)

Keller, Thomas, *The French Laundry Cookbook* (London, 1999)

Khonkhai, Khammaan, trans. Gehan Wijeyewardene, *The Teachers of Mad Dog Swamp* [1978] (Chiang Mai, 1992)

King, J.C.H., Birgit Pautsztat and Robert Storrie, *Arctic Clothing* (Montreal, 2005)

Kitchiner, William, *Apicius Redivivus* (London, 1817)

Kritzman, Lawrence D., *Food: A Culinary History* (New York, 1996)

Larousse Gastronomique (New York, 2001)

Lo, Vivienne, 'Pleasure, Prohibition and Pain: Food and Medicine in Traditional China', in *Tripod and Palate*, ed. Roel Sterckx (New York, 2005)

Luard, Elisabeth, *The Latin American Kitchen* (London, 2002)

McLagan, Jennifer, *Odd Bits: How to Cook the Rest of the Animal* (New York, 2011)

—, *How to Cook the Rest of the Animal* (London, 2011)

McNamee, Gregory, *Moveable Feasts: The History, Science, and the Lore of Food* (Westport, CT, 2007)

Mallos, Tess, *The Complete Middle East Cookbook* (London, 1995)

Markham, Gervase, *The English Hus-wife* (1615)

Marks, Gil, *The Encyclopedia of Jewish Food* (Princeton, NJ, 2010)

Mennell, Stephen, *All Manners of Food: Eating and Taste in England and France from the Middle Ages to the Present* [1985] (Chicago, IL, 1996)

Michalik, Eva, *The Food and Cooking of Poland* (London, 2008)

Miller, Jonathan, *The Body in Question* [1980] (London, 2000)

Miller, William Ian, *The Anatomy of Disgust* (Cambridge, MA, 1997)

Parker-Bowles, Tom, *The Year of Living Dangerously* (London, 2008)

Patten, Marguerite, *Post-war Kitchen* (London, 1998)

Phillips, Denise, *New Flavours of the Jewish Table* (London, 2008)

Philpott, T., 'Flesh and Bone', *Gastronomica*, VII/2 (2007)

Platina, Bartholomaeus de, *Concerning Honest Pleasures and Physical Well-being* (1474)

Polo, Marco, and Henry Yule, trans. and ed., *The Book of Ser Marco Polo, the Venetian: Concerning the Kingdoms and the Marvels of the East* (Cambridge, 1999)

Powell, Julie, *Cleaving* (London, 2009)

Rögnvaldardóttir, Nanna, *Icelandic Food and Cookery*, (New York, 2002)

Root, Waverley, *The Food of France* [1958] (London, 1983)

Schwabe, Calvin W., *Unmentionable Cuisine* (Charlottesville, VA, 1979)

Scruton, Roger, 'Eating the World' (2003), at www.opendemocracy. net, last accessed 1 May 2012

Searles, Edmund, 'Food and the Making of Modern Inuit Identities', *Food and Foodways: History and Culture of Human Nourishment*, 10 (2002)

Smith, Eliza, *The Compleat Housewife* (London, 1727)

Strong, Jeremy, 'The Modern Offal Eaters', *Gastronomica*, VI/2 (2006)

Thayer, Bill, ed., *Historia Augusta* [1924], available online at www. penelope.uchicago.edu, last accessed 1 May 2012

Toussaint-Samat, Maguelonne, *History of Food*, trans. Anthea Bell (London, 1987)

Tsuji, Shizuo, and M.F.K. Fisher, *Japanese Cooking: A Simple Art* (New York, 1998)

Ubaldi, Jack, and Elizabeth Crossman, *Jack Ubaldi's Meat Book* (New York, 1991)

Van Esterik, *Food Culture in Southeast Asia* (London, 2008)

Weaver, Tara Austen, *The Butcher and the Vegetarian* (New York, 2010)

Wheeler, Douglas L., *Historical Dictionary of Portugal* (Lanham, MD, 1994)

Websites and Associations

Offal Good
Chef Chris Consentino's educational website about offal
www.offalgood.com

Eat Me Daily
General critical food blog with Offal of the Week column
www.eatmedaily.com

The Food Maven
Restaurant critic Arthur Schwartz's food blog
www.thefoodmaven.com

Save the Deli
David Sax's website about the Jewish delicatessen
www.savethedeli.com

The Philosophy of Food Project
University of Texas site on the philosophical significance
of food, director David M. Kaplan
www.food.unt.edu/philfood

The Food Timeline
www.foodtimeline.org

Acknowledgements

Thanks to Sue Best, Sally Bjork, Som Chewasuwan, Zhenya Dewfield of EBLEX, Stephanie Diani, Ruth Dupré, Jeremy Edwards, Peter Edwards, The European Supermarket West Ealing, Sue Floyd, Brenda Gentle, Jan Göransson of The Swedish Film Institute, Jonathan Goy of World Trade Statistics, Irene Gunston, Görel Halström, Anissa Helou, Susan Huntington, The International Meat Trade Association, Roger Kelsey of The National Federation of Meat and Food Traders, Kate Kessling, Michael Leaman, Oliver Leaman, Tony Luckhurst, Kate Lynch, Salma Malik, Stephen Martyn, Tony Matelli, Bruce McCall, Lynne Olver of The Food Timeline, Chris Peake, Sheila Perkins, Jane Reddish, Richardson's Butchers Northfields, Quality Meat Scotland, Alex Rushmer, Nicole Russo of Leo Koenig Inc., Gordon Sloan, Kari Smith, Olive Smith, John Vassallo, Dick Vigers, Waitrose and Tara Austen Weaver.

Photo Acknowledgements

The author and the publishers wish to express their thanks to the below sources of illustrative material and/or permission to reproduce it:

Author's collection: pp. 8, 16–17, 21, 28, 37, 38, 45, 58, 72, 74, 80–81, 97, 107; Shutterstock: pp. 6, 11, 31, 32, 33, 34, 35, 40, 48, 49, 53, 59, 61, 63, 73, 85; Michael Leaman: pp. 64, 65, 66–7; *Le Boucher* (dir. Claude Chabrol, 1970): p. 71; Stephanie Diani: pp. 77, 78; *Silent Witness* (dir. Noella Smith, 1996): p. 101; British Museum: pp. 9, 18, 44, 56, 100; Victoria & Albert Museum: pp. 13, 89, 108; Ruth Dupre: p. 20; Rex Features: p. 50; Kate Lynch: p. 84; Huntington Archive: p. 93.

Index

italic numbers refer to illustrations; **bold** to recipes

Absolutely Fabulous 106
America
    North 22, 43–7
    South 40–41
Amish 46
Apicius 10–11, 12, 51, 79
Armenia 39
Australia 44, 47, 48
    dugong *49*
Austria 53, 54

battalia pie **111**
Beeton, (Mrs) Isabella 27, 57,
    112
Bierce, Ambrose, *The Devil's
    Dictionary* 96
black pudding 10–11, 44, 54
    blackpot 79
    blood cakes 32
    blood pudding *56*, 65, **110**;
    soup 30, 52
    drisheen 18
    farinbato 62, 65
    see also haggis
blood 10, 11, 12, 13, 15, 71, 79

dinuguan 36
    Masai 94
    Inuit 94–5
Blumenthal, Heston 85–6
Boucher, Le (Claude Chabrol)
    70
Bradley, James, *Flyboys* 92–3
brains 11, 37–8, 51, 62, 64, 99
    beef 79
    fritters **115**
    lamb 29, 85
    monkey 94
    in ravioli 41
    sparrow 79
    in vine leaves 39
brawn 15, 43, 55, 64, 65
    blewe manger **110**
    pig 39
    potted *heid* 68
    sandwich 46
Burns, Robert 83
butchery 19, *20*, 60, 75, 76, 79

cannibalism 88, 91–3
Carême, Antonin 51, 83

China 21, 30–34, 47, 94
    medicine 100–02
Chittenden, Hiram Martin,
    The American Fur Trade of
    the Far West 45
Clarke, Harry, *Apparition of the*
    Sacred Heart 89
Cobbett, William 57
Consentino, Chris 22
Corbier, Mireille 14
Coren, Giles 81
Creutzfeldt-Jakob disease
    104
Cyprus 39, *85*

Daniels, Sarah, *Gut Girls* 75
David, Elizabeth 26
Davidson, Alan 82
Decameron, The 91
Depardieu, Gérard 70
Diani, Stephanie, *Offal Taste*
    76–8
Dickens, Charles *Oliver Twist*
    75–6
Douglas, Mary 25
Douglas, Norman, *Venus in the*
    Kitchen 78–9
dugong *49*
Dumas, Alexandre 48, 52
Dunlop, Fuchsia 21, 33
Dupré, Ruth, *Butchery 20*

Egypt, tomb paintings 8–9
Elagabalus, emperor 12–13
erotic offal 43, 76, 78–9, 85
Escoffier, Auguste 52, 59, **115**

Ethiopia, hyena-men 87–8

Farrell, J. G., *The Siege of*
    Krishnapur 72–3
France 22, 48–53, 60, 62

Galen 10, 11, 96, 99, 100,
    102
Germany 52, 53–4
giblets 20, 62
    alicot 51
    turkey 52, **113**
Good Housewives' Closet, The
    55
Greece 8, 39, 87, 96

haggis 82–3
Hardy, Thomas 79
Haroutunian, Arto der 40
harslet **113**
head 12, 13, 15, 51, 61
    calf 39
    chicken 98
    duck 31
    fish 33
    pig 39, 65, 85
    sheep 37, 40, 66, 68
heart 8, 11, 15, 23, 30, 53, 55,
    62
    calf **114**
    frog 36
    kebab 37
    pig 77
    Sacred Heart 88–90
    sheep 38, *74*
Helou, Anissa 37–8

Henderson, Fergus 22–3, 29
Hieatt, Constance B., and
    Sharon Butler 19
Hippocrates 10
Houston, Douglas, *With the
    Offal Eaters* 22
humours, the 23, 96, 99, 100

iftar 39
India 36–7, *49*; Siege of
    Krishnapur 72
Indonesia 36
intestines 11, 12, 18, 23, 31,
    38–9, 92, 99
    Association Amicale des
    Amateurs d'Andouillette
    Authentique 53
    beef 35
    chitterlings 43, 46
    lamb and veal 62
    marsupial 47
    pajata 62
    pork 34, 35
    raincoats 106
    sheep 37
Iran 37, *40*
Israel 55
Italy 59, 60–63

Japan 27, 35–6
    cannibalism 92–4
    fugu 104–5
    Shintoism 90
Jews, Judaism 46, 54–5, 101
Joyce, James 54

kale pache 37
Keller, Thomas 68
kidneys 8, 11, 18, 23, 24, 26,
    34, 39, 43, 54, 62, 79,
    99
    devilled **120**
    Inuit 95
    pork 32, 33, 59
    sheep 51
    steak and kidney pudding
    59
Kirchof, Hans Wilhelm 54
kokoretsi 39

Laos 34
Lebanon 37
Lévi-Strauss, Claude 92
Leviticus 11, 90
Lewis, Norman 98
liver 99–100
    goose liver 10, 11, 12,
    54
    Liver Lovers' Club 46
    see also pâté
Lotar, Eli 74
Luard, Elizabeth, *The Latin
    American Kitchen* 41
lungs 11, 15, 26, 38, 39, 54, 58,
    62, 82, 92, 99
Lynch, Kate *The Runner in the
    Slaughterhouse* 84

Markham, Gervase, *The
    English Hus-wife* 102
marrow 11, 15, 27, 41, 43, 45,
    53, 55

osso buco 61, 62
    marrow pudding **110**
Mexico 40, 97
Miller, Jonathan 24, 27
milt 15, 54, 58
Molokhovet, Elena, *A Gift to
    Young Housewives* 39
mythological beliefs 92
    vampires 94

Nepal 37
New Zealand 44, 48
Normans, the 55
noumbles **109**

Orsi, Pierre 22
oxtail 35, 47, 77, **114**

pâté
    de foie gras 10–11, *45*, 51,
    115
    roasted **116**
    Strasbourg 96
pemmican 45
Petronius, *Satyricon* 83–4
Philippines 36; *Iglesia ni Cristo* 90
pig organ soup **120**
placenta 103
Polo, Marco 30, 60
Portugal 62
Powell, Julie 76
Pym, Barbara 75
Pythagoras 11–12

rawness 7, 20, 21, 30, 34, 37,
    68, 82, 103
Reynolds, Victoria 74

Russia 39, 107
    Buriats 68
Sandby, Paul, *Any Tripe or
    Calves Feet 18*
Scandinavia 63–8
    Inuit 95
Scruton, Roger 23
Second World War, the 41, 60,
    107
Shakespeare, William
    Hamlet 19
    The Merchant of Venice 90
Singapore 35
South Korea 34
Spain 60, 62, 70
spleen 15, 36, 54, 61, 62, 99
    splinatero 19
sweetbreads 15, 18, 20, 26, 40,
    51, 53, 54, 58, 99
    fritto misto 62
    pajata 62, **111–12**

Tacuinum Sanitatis 60
Taillevent, *Le Viandier* 51
testicles 15, 18, 37, 62, 65, 70,
    76, 85
    lamb stones **111–12**
    Testicle Festivals, regional
    46
Thailand 34, **120**
tripe 11, 13, 15, 18, 20, 24, 26,
    27, 32, 35, 37, 38, 39, 41,
    48, 81
    calf 98, **109**
    lampredotto 63, 99
    à la mode de Caen 50
    pieds et pacquets 51, 54

trotters 15, 37, 39, 41, 51
    pettitoes, pig's **112–13**
    à la Sainte Menehould 52,
    62–3
Turkey 38–9

Ubaldi, Jack *Meat Book* 47
udder 13, 15, 19, 39, 53, 54
UK 55–60, 103
umami 25–6
umbles 55
Unani (Unani-tibbi) 96

Vietnam 25, 35, 81
Vikramaditya Cooked for Kali 93

Weaver, Tara Austen 23
Weenix, Jan Baptist, *Pig's*
    Carcasse 13
Wensley, Mary-Anne 106
Wirgman, John *44*
Wodehouse, P. G., *Mulliner*
    Nights 75